IMPACT Intervention Year 5

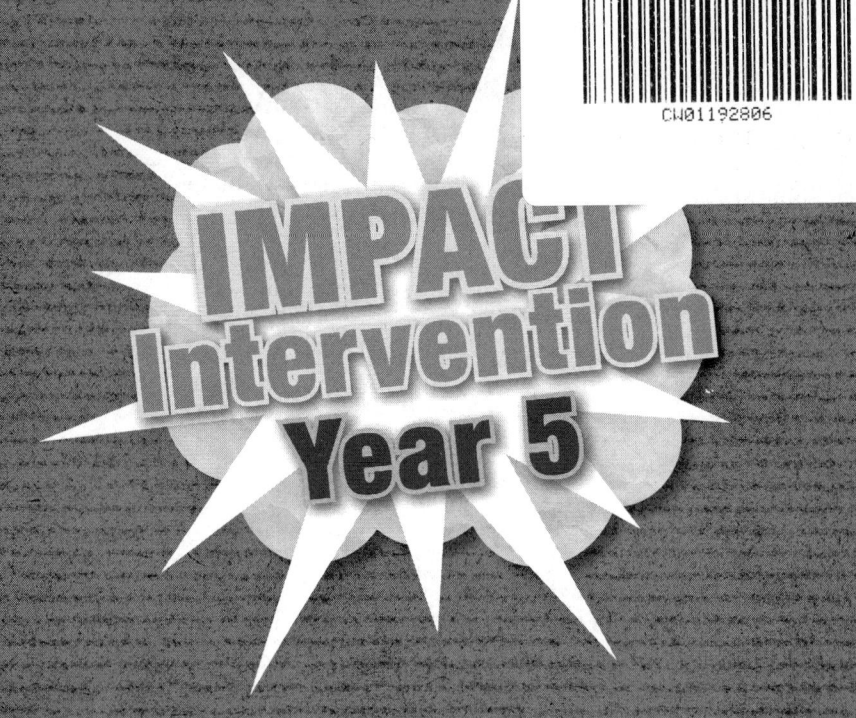

Caroline Clissold and Shelley Welsh

Published by Keen Kite Books
An imprint of HarperCollins*Publishers* Ltd
The News Building
1 London Bridge Street
London
SE1 9GF

Text and design © 2017 Keen Kite Books, an imprint of HarperCollins*Publishers* Ltd

10 9 8 7 6 5 4 3 2 1

ISBN 978-0-00-823847-6

The author asserts their moral right to be identified as the author of this work.

Any educational institution that has purchased one copy of this publication may make duplicate copies for use exclusively within that institution. Permission does not extend to reproduction, storage in a retrieval system or transmission in any form or by any means – electronic, mechanical, photocopying, recording or otherwise – of duplicate copies for lending, renting or selling to any other user or institution without the prior consent, in writing, of the Publisher.

British Library Cataloguing in Publication Data

A catalogue record for this publication is available from the British Library.

Authors: Caroline Clissold and Shelley Welsh
Commissioning Editors: Shelley Teasdale and Michelle l'Anson
Project Manager: Fiona Watson
Editor: Becki Adlard
Internal design and illustrations: QBS Learning
Production: Lyndsey Rogers

Introduction

Impact Intervention is a new series of resources created by teachers and aimed at teaching assistants, classroom assistants, NQTs and time-strapped teachers.

The books include tried and tested ready-to-go activities that are intended for use with small groups of pupils to help scaffold learning.

The resources can be used to deliver pre-teach sessions, booster interventions or breakout sessions after lessons to pick up pupils who are struggling to achieve a learning outcome.

Impact Intervention can be dipped into as needed and used with minimal preparation.

The books contain:
- standalone sessions with activities that focus on an achievable part of a learning objective
- content that has been broken down into small steps so that it is easy to follow and deliver
- activities that can be easily implemented in a 15–20-minute session without the need to read through lots of information in advance
- probing questions, prompts and key checks to help assess pupils' knowledge and understanding
- support and extension ideas.

Each title in the series contains content that is robust, age-appropriate and adheres to the standard of the KS1 / KS2 English and maths programmes of study.

Contents

Number – number and place value

The 2 Rs!	6
What's my value?	8
Order, order	10
Comparisons	12
Round it	16
The Romans	21

Number – addition and subtraction

Addition and subtraction	30
Sequencing	31
More sequencing	32
Rounding and adjusting	33
Counting on	34
Problems with money	35
Problems with length	36
Problems with mass	37
Problems with capacity	38
Problems with volume	39
Problems with time	40

Number – multiplication and division

Multiples and factors	41
All about primes	42
Prime or not?	43
Multiplication	44
Using known facts	45
Division	46
Squares and cubes	47
Scaling	48

Number – fractions

More 2 Rs!	7
Thousandths	9
More ordering	11
More comparisons	13
Powers of 10	14
Brrr!	15
Round it again	17
And again!	18
Problems, problems	19
More problems	20
Turning decimals to fractions	22
Equivalences	23
Comparing fractions	24
Mix them up	25
Add and subtract	26
Multiply	27
Percentages	28
Yet more problems	29

Measurement

Problems with money	35
Problems with length	36
Problems with mass	37
Problems with capacity	38
Problems with volume	39
Problems with time	40

Writing – vocabulary, grammar and punctuation

Degrees of possibility	50
Relative clauses I	51
Relative clauses II	52
Cohesion I	53
Cohesion II	55
Cohesion III	56
Tense consistency I	57
Tense consistency II	58
Past perfect	59
Modal verbs	60
Commas	61
Brackets, dashes and commas	62

Writing – transcription

Prefixes dis- and mis-	63
Prefixes de-, re- and over-	64
Prefixes that come from Latin and Greek	65
Suffixes I	66
Suffixes II	67
Morphology and etymology	68

Silent letters	70
Homophones	71
Near homophones and tricky homophones	73
Exception words	75
Dictionary work	77
More dictionary work	78
Thesaurus work	80

Reading – comprehension

Information texts	82
Persuasive letters	83
Adverts	84
Newspaper reports	85
Recounts	86

Writing – composition

Writing an information text	87
Writing persuasive letters	89
Writing adverts	91
Writing newspaper reports	92
Writing recounts	94
Proofreading to improve	96

IMPACT Intervention Maths Activities

The 2 Rs!

Strand: Number – number and place value

Learning objective: To read and write numbers to at least 1 000 000.

You will need: digit cards, place value grids (millions to ones)

1. Give each pupil a set of digit cards. Ask them to lay the cards in a line in order from zero to nine. **Say:** *Show me nine. Can you double it? Show me the new number. How did you do that?* Accept and clarify suggestions. **Say:** *Double 18. What strategy did you use? Is there another way to double 18?* (e.g. partition 18 into 10 and 8, double both, recombine, double 20 and subtract 4) **Say:** *Add nine onto 36. How did you do that? Is there another way?* (e.g. add 10, subtract one, partition 9 into 4 and 5, add 4 to 36 to make 40, then add 5) **Say:** *Double 45. How did you do that?*

2. Pupils put the 90 they made above on the table away from the other cards. **Say:** *Make 90 read 290. Make 290 read 2907. What is the role of the zero?* (place holder, holding the place of the tens) **Say:** *Make 2907 read 29 076. What position is zero holding now? Make 29 076 read 290 763. What position is zero holding now? Make 290 763 read 8 290 763. What position is zero holding now?*

3. Using the 8 290 763 they have made, ask pupils to swap pairs of digits (e.g. 8 and 7). **Ask:** *Is the number greater or smaller? Roughly how much smaller?* (one million) **Say:** *Read the number.*

4. Repeat step 3 a few times, asking pupils to swap digits in different positions. Each time, ask whether the number is greater or smaller and by how much. Each time, ask pupils to read the new number.

5. Call out numbers with at least one zero for pupils to write down (e.g. two million, three hundred and forty-one thousand, five hundred and eighty). Each time, ask pupils to tell you the role of the zero.

Key checks: Do pupils understand the role of zero as a place holder?

Extension: Ask pupils to make seven-digit numbers using their digit cards for a partner to read.

Support: Use place value grids (millions to ones). Pupils place digit cards in each position and use the heading on the grids to help them read the number.

More 2 Rs!

Strand: Number – fractions (including decimals and percentages)

Learning objective: To read and write numbers with up to three decimal places.

You will need: digit cards, place value grids with hundreds, tens, ones, tenths, hundredths and thousandths positions

1. Give each pupil a set of digit cards and a place value grid. Ask them to place 3 in the hundreds, 7 in the tens, 4 in the ones and 6 in the tenths. **Ask:** *What is the digit 3 worth? How do you know? What is the digit 4 worth? How do you know? What is the digit 6 worth? How do you know? What is the digit 7 worth? How do you know? Can you read the whole number?* (three hundred and seventy-four and six tenths) *Is there another way to say this number?* (three hundred and seventy-four point six) *What is the role of the decimal point? Can you explain in a different way?* (e.g. separates the whole numbers from the decimal)

2. Repeat for other numbers with tenths only.

3. Pupils place 6 in the hundreds, 9 in the tens, 2 in the ones, 8 in the tenths and 5 in the hundredths. Ask them to explain what each digit is worth and how they know. They then read the whole number. Repeat for other numbers with tenths and hundredths.

4. Repeat the process for numbers with tenths, hundredths and thousandths. **Ask:** *Are tenths greater or smaller than thousandths? How do you know?* (Greater because they are the parts of one when one has been divided into 10 parts; thousandths are the parts of one when one has been divided into 1000 parts.)

5. Call out numbers with tenths, tenths and hundredths and then tenths, hundredths and thousandths for pupils to write down.

Key checks: Do pupils understand the role of the decimal point?

Extension: Ask pupils to make three-digit numbers with three decimal places using their digit cards for a partner to read.

Support: Focus on single-digit numbers with tenths initially. Give pupils lots of practice. Gradually include hundredths and then, if appropriate, thousandths.

What's my value?

Strand: Number – number and place value

Learning objective: To determine the value of each digit to at least 1 000 000.

You will need: digit cards, place value grids (millions to ones)

1. Give each pupil a set of digit cards and a place value grid. **Say:** *Make 42 in your grid. What can you tell me about the digit 4? What else?* Guide pupils to work out that four is in the tens position and must be multiplied by 10 to give its true value of 40. *What can you tell me about the digit 2?* Together say, two is in the ones position and must be multiplied by one to give its true value of two.

2. **Say:** *Make 742 in your grid. What can you tell me about the digit 7? What else?* Guide pupils to work out that seven is positioned in the hundreds position and must be multiplied by 100 to give its true value of 700.

3. **Say:** *Make 8742 in your grid. What can you tell me about the digit 8? What else?* Guide pupils to work out that eight is positioned in the thousands position and must be multiplied by 1000 to give its true value of 8000.

4. Repeat for 38 742, 138 742 and 5 138 742. **Ask:** *What can you tell me about the digit 3/1/5? What else?* Guide pupils to work out that three is positioned in the tens of thousands position and must be multiplied by 10 000 to give its true value of 30 000 / one is positioned in the hundreds of thousands position and must be multiplied by 100 000 to give 100 000 / five is positioned in the millions position and must be multiplied by one million to give 5 000 000.

5. Repeat the process for other millions numbers.

Key checks: Do pupils understand the positional and multiplicative aspects of place value?

Extension: Ask pupils to make up their own number and to give a written explanation of where each digit is positioned and what is done to it to give its true value.

Support: Begin with thousands numbers and explore the positional and multiplicative aspects of each digit and gradually build up to millions, if appropriate.

Thousandths

Strand: Number – fractions (including decimals and percentages)

Learning objective: To recognise and use thousandths and relate them to tenths, hundredths and decimal equivalents.

You will need: digit cards, place value grids with thousandths to hundreds positions

1. Give each pupil a set of digit cards and a place value grid. **Say:** *Make 467 in your grid. What can you tell me about the digit 4? What else?* Guide pupils to work out that four is in the hundreds position and must be multiplied by 100 to give its true value of 400. **Ask:** *What can you tell me about the digit 6? What else?* Guide pupils to work out that six is in the tens position and must be multiplied by 10 to give its true value of 60. **Ask:** *What can you tell me about the digit 7?* Guide pupils to work out that seven is in the ones position and must be multiplied by one to give its true value of seven.

2. **Say:** *Make 467 and 3 tenths in your grid. What can you tell me about the digit 3? What else?* Guide pupils to work out that three is in the tenths position and must be multiplied by 1 tenth to give its true value of 3 tenths. **Ask:** *Is there another way to say 467 and 3 tenths?* Together say, 467 and 3 tenths is equivalent to 467 point 3. **Ask:** *What is the role of the point?* (It is a decimal point separating the whole number from the decimal.)

3. **Say:** *Make 467, 3 tenths and 8 hundredths in your grid. What can you tell me about the digit 8? What else?* Guide pupils to work out that eight is positioned in the hundredths position and must be multiplied by 1 hundredth to give its true value of 8 hundredths. **Ask:** *Is there another way to say 467, 3 tenths and 8 hundredths?* Together say, 467, 3 tenths and 8 hundredths is equivalent to 467 point three eight.

4. Repeat for 467, 3 tenths, 8 hundredths and 9 thousandths.

5. Repeat for other three-digit numbers with three decimal places.

Key checks: Do pupils understand the link between the fractions to thousandths and equivalent decimals?

Extension: Ask pupils to make their own number and explain the positional and multiplicative aspects of place value.

Support: Focus on tenths, exploring the link between the fraction and decimal.

Order, order

Strand: Number – number and place value

Learning objective: To order numbers to at least 1 000 000.

You will need: whiteboard, whiteboard pen, digit cards, place value grids (millions to ones)

1. Give each pupil two sets of digit cards and a place value grid. **Say:** *Make 1 678 294 in your grid. What can you tell me about each digit? What else?* Pupils should explain that a digit is placed in a position and multiplied by the value of that position to give the real value of the number.

2. **Say:** *Make 1 871 325 underneath your first number.* **Ask:** *What can you tell me about each digit? What else?* Pupils should explain the positional and multiplicative aspects of place value for each digit.

3. **Ask:** *Which of your numbers is the greater? How do you know?* (the millions are the same, so pupils need to look at the 100 000 number) *Which digits are in the 100 000 position in both your numbers?* (6 and 8) *What value does each digit have?* (600 000 and 800 000) *Do we need to look at the other values? Why not?* (800 000 is greater than 600 000, so 1 871 325 is the greater number.)

4. **Ask:** *Can you rearrange the digits that make 1 871 325 so that this number is less than 1 678 294? What have you done? How do you know it is less? Did anyone do anything different?*

5. Write three of the pupils' new numbers on the board. **Ask:** *Which of these is the least? How do you know? Which is the greatest? How do you know? Read the numbers in order from least to greatest.*

6. Repeat for other numbers with one in the millions position.

Key checks: Do pupils understand how to order numbers when identical digits are in the same position?

Extension: Ask pupils to write down three or four numbers that have the same millions, 100 000 and 10 000 digits. They order these according to the size of the thousands digits.

Support: Focus on ordering according to the millions numbers. When confident, keep these the same so pupils order according to the 100 000 digits.

More ordering

Strand: Number – fractions (including decimals and percentages)

Learning objective: To order numbers with up to three decimal places.

You will need: whiteboard, whiteboard pen, digit cards, place value grids with hundreds to thousandths positions

1. Give each pupil two sets of digit cards and a place value grid. **Say:** *Make 492.6 in your grid. What can you tell me about each digit? What else?* Pupils should explain that a digit is placed in a position and multiplied by the value of that position to give the real value of the number.

2. **Say:** *Make 492.1 underneath your first number. What can you tell me about each digit? What else?* Pupils should explain the positional and multiplicative aspects of place value for each digit.

3. **Ask:** *Which of your numbers is the greatest? How do you know?* (the digits in the whole number positions are the same, so pupils need to look at the tenths) *Which digits are in the tenths position in both your numbers?* (6 and 1) *What value does each digit have?* ($\frac{6}{10}$ and $\frac{1}{10}$) *Which number is the greater? How do you know?* Guide pupils to work out that 492.6 is greater than 492.1 because it has a greater number of tenths.

4. **Ask:** *Can you rearrange the digits that make 492.6 so that this number is less than 492.1? What have you done? How do you know it is less? Did anyone do anything different?*

5. Write three of the pupils' new numbers on the board. **Ask:** *Which of these is the least? How do you know? Which is the greatest? How do you know? Read the numbers in order from least to greatest.*

6. Repeat for other numbers with tenths. Repeat for three-digit numbers with two and then three decimal places.

Key checks: Do pupils understand how to order decimal numbers when identical digits are in the same position?

Extension: Ask pupils to write down three or four three-digit numbers that have the same digits in the first four positions (e.g. 456.392, 456.328). They order these according to the size of the hundredths.

Support: Focus on ordering according to tenths. When confident, pupils order according to hundredths and then thousandths digits.

Comparisons

Strand: Number – number and place value

Learning objective: To compare numbers to at least 1 000 000.

You will need: whiteboard, whiteboard pen, digit cards, place value grids (millions to ones), coloured counters (red = 1 000 000, blue = 100 000, green = 10 000, orange = 1 000, yellow = 100, pink = 10, brown = 1)

1. Give each pupil two sets of digit cards and a place value grid. **Say:** *Make 3 876 249 in your grid. What can you tell me about each digit? What else?* Pupils should explain that a digit is placed in a position and multiplied by the value of that position to give the real value of the number.

2. **Say:** *Make 2 653 123 underneath your first number. What can you tell me about each digit? What else?* Pupils should explain the positional and multiplicative aspects of place value for each digit.

3. **Ask:** *Which of your numbers is the greater? How do you know?* (3 876 249: there is one more million)

4. **Ask:** *Which symbol do we use for greater than? Which symbol do we use for less than? How can we compare our two numbers using these symbols?* Ask pupils to write the numbers on the board using > and then <.

5. Ask pupils to make the two numbers using coloured counters. **Ask:** *How can we make them equal?* Pupils explore, using the counters, what they need to take from the larger number to make the smaller number. They record: 3 876 249 − 1 223 126 = 2 653 123. Can they reason that they would need to add the number taken from the larger number to make the smaller number equal to the larger number? (3 876 249 = 2 653 123 + 1 223 126)

6. Repeat for other pairs of seven-digit numbers where the second number has digits that are smaller than the first number in each position.

Key checks: Do pupils understand the use of > and <?

Extension: Ask pupils to make up seven-digit numbers to compare using >, < and =.

Support: Focus on comparing using > and <.

More comparisons

Strand: Number – fractions (including decimals and percentages)

Learning objective: To compare numbers with up to three decimal places.

You will need: whiteboard, whiteboard pen, digit cards, place value grids with hundreds to thousandths positions, coloured counters (red = 100, blue = 10, green = 1, orange = tenth, yellow = hundredth, brown = thousandth)

1. Give each pupil two sets of digit cards and a place value grid. **Say:** *Make 784.2 in your grid. What can you tell me about each digit? What else?* Pupils should explain that a digit is placed in a position and multiplied by the value of that position to give the real value of the number.

2. **Say:** *Make 651.1 underneath your first number. What can you tell me about each digit? What else?* Pupils should explain the positional and multiplicative aspects of place value for each digit.

3. **Ask:** *Which of your numbers is the greater? How do you know?* (784.2: there is one more hundred)

4. **Ask:** *How can we compare our two numbers using the greater than and less than symbols?* Ask pupils to write the numbers on the board using > and then <.

5. Ask pupils to make the two numbers using coloured counters. **Ask:** *How can we make them equal?* Pupils explore, using the counters, what they need to take from the larger number to make the smaller number. They record: 784.2 − 133.1 = 651.1. They then explore what they need to add to the smaller number in order for it to equal the greater number and record: 784.2 = 651.1 + 133.1.

6. Repeat for other pairs of three-digit numbers with one, then two and three decimal places. The second number must have digits that are smaller than the first number in each position.

Key checks: Do pupils accurately use > and <?

Extension: Ask pupils to make up three-digit numbers with three decimal places to compare using >, < and =.

Support: Focus on comparing using > and <.

Powers of 10

Strand: Number – fractions (including decimals), multiplication and division

Learning objectives: To count forwards or backwards in steps of powers of 10 for any given number up to 1 000 000. To multiply and divide whole numbers and those involving decimals by 10, 100 and 1000.

You will need: a counting stick, digit cards (extra zero cards), place value grids from millions to hundredths positions

1. Show the counting stick.
   Ask: *If zero is at this end and 100 is at the other, what steps will we be counting in?* Together count in tens from zero to 100 and back to zero.
   Ask: *If zero is at this end and 1000 is at the other, what steps will we be counting in?* Together count in hundreds from zero to 1000 and back to zero. Repeat for 10 000 counting in thousands, 100 000 counting in ten thousands and one million counting in hundred thousands.
   Ask: *What do you notice?* (The pattern is very similar.) Introduce the idea of counting in powers of 10 (100s are 10 times greater than 10s, 1000s are 10 times greater than 100s and so on).

2. Give each pupil a set of digit cards, extra zero cards and a place value grid.
   Say: *Make 34 in your grid. Now multiply it by 10. What have you done?* (made the number 10 times bigger, moved the 3 tens to 3 hundreds, 4 ones to 4 tens, placed zero as a place holder in the ones) *Now multiply it by 10 again. What have you done?* (made the number 10 times bigger again) *Now divide 3400 by 10. What do you notice?* (10 times smaller, back to 340) *Now divide 340 by 10. What do you notice?* (10 times smaller, back to 34)

3. **Say:** *Multiply 34 by 100. What have you done?* (made the number 100 times bigger, moved the 3 tens to 3 thousands, 4 ones to 4 hundreds, placed zero as a place holder in the tens and ones) *What do you notice?* (multiplying by 100 is the same as multiplying by 10 and 10 again) Repeat for dividing by 100 and then multiplying and dividing by 1000. Repeat for other numbers.

Key checks: Do pupils talk about adding zeros when multiplying by powers of 10? This is incorrect. They should be thinking in terms of the digits becoming 10/100 times greater.

Extension: Ask pupils to make up their own numbers to multiply and divide by 10, 100 and 1000.

Support: Focus on multiplying and dividing by 10.

Brrr!

Strand: Number – fractions (including decimals and percentages)

Learning objective: To interpret negative numbers in context, count forwards and backwards with positive and negative whole numbers, including through zero.

You will need: a counting stick, a post-it note labelled zero

1. Show the counting stick vertically with zero in the middle.
   Ask: *If we are counting in ones, which numbers will be at the ends of my stick?* Together, count in ones from the zero to five. Count in ones from five to negative five.
   Ask: *If we are counting in twos, which numbers will be at the ends of my stick?* (10 and –10) Together, count in twos from negative 10 to 10.
   Ask: *If we are counting in threes, which numbers will be at the ends of my stick?* (15 and –15) Together, count in threes from one end of the stick to the other.
   Ask: *How can you work out which numbers go at either end of the stick when we count in any steps?* Multiply the step size by five, because the ends are the fifth intervals.

2. **Ask:** *Where do we find negative numbers in real life?* Elicit some examples (e.g. temperature, land below sea level, bank accounts). Discuss what each of these are and any other suggestions pupils might make.

3. Treat the counting stick as a thermometer. Point to the end that is positive.
   Say: *The temperature is 10°C. If it falls by 14 degrees, what number will it show? If it now rises by 8 degrees, what number will it show?* Repeat questioning like this, changing the step size to three, four and five.

4. Repeat for the context of metres above and below sea level with the step sizes in 100 and 1000.

5. Repeat for the context of bank accounts with the step sizes in 50 and 150.

Key checks: Do pupils say, for example, minus 8 for a negative? The word negative should be used. You might need to explain that although people often talk about temperatures using minus, or sea level by saying degrees below sea level, this is inaccurate and the word negative should be used.

Extension: Ask pupils to make up their own temperature increase and decrease problems to give to a partner to solve.

Support: Focus on simple step sizes for counting below zero for example 4, 2, 0, -2, -4.

Round it

Strand: Number – number and place value

Learning objective: To round any number up to 1 000 000 to the nearest 10, 100, 1000, 10 000 and 100 000.

You will need: laminated empty number lines with 10 marked divisions

1. **Ask:** *What does it mean to round a number up or down? Can anyone explain in a different way? Why is rounding helpful? Can you give another reason?* (e.g. if we don't need an exact answer, only an estimate) *How would we know when to round up?* (If the number is 5, 50, 500 or more.) *How would we know when to round down?* (If the number is less than 5, 50, 500.)

2. Call out different numbers and pupils put their thumbs up if the number needs rounding up or their thumbs down if the number needs rounding down.

3. Give pupils an empty number line. **Say:** *Write 560 at one end and 570 at the other. Circle the division where 565 would be. Which numbers would be rounded up to 570? How do you know? Which numbers would be rounded down to 560? How do you know?*

4. **Say:** *Write 3500 at one end and 3600 at the other. Circle the division where 3550 would be. Where would 3568 go on your number line? How do you know? If you needed to round 3568 to the nearest 100, what number would that be? How do you know?*

5. Repeat for different numbers that come between 3500 and 3600, first rounding to 100 and then to 1000.

6. Repeat for:
   - 3000 at one end and 4000 at the other and round to the nearest 1000
   - 30 000 and 40 000 and round to the nearest 10 000
   - 300 000 and 400 000 and round to the nearest 100 000
   - 3 000 000 and 4 000 000 and round to the nearest million.

Key checks: Do pupils understand the importance of rounding for approximating? Do they know which digit to look at in order to round up or down?

Extension: Ask pupils to make up their own millions numbers to give to a partner to round.

Support: Focus on rounding to 10, 100 and 1000 until confident and then move on to higher numbers, if appropriate.

Round it again

Strand: Number – fractions (including decimals and percentages)

Learning objective: To round decimals with two decimal places to the nearest whole number.

You will need: laminated empty number lines with 10 marked divisions

1. **Ask:** *What does it mean to round a whole number? Can you explain in a different way? Why is rounding helpful?* (e.g. if we don't need an exact answer, only an estimate) *How would we know when to round up?* (if the number is 5, 50, 500 or more) *How would we know when to round down?* (if the number is less than 5, 50, 500) *What do you think it means to round a number with decimal places?* (it is exactly the same as rounding whole numbers) *How do you think we would round 5.2 to the nearest whole number?* (round down because the number is less than 5.5) *What is 5.2 rounded to the nearest whole number?* (5) *What about 5.7?* (6)

2. Call out different numbers (e.g. 5.1, 5.8, 5.5). Pupils put their thumbs up if the number needs rounding up or their thumbs down if the number needs rounding down.

3. Give pupils an empty number line. **Say:** *Write 5 at one end and 6 at the other. Circle the division where 5.5 would be. Which numbers would be rounded up to 6? How do you know? Which numbers would be rounded down to 5? How do you know?*

4. **Say:** *Write 15 at one end and 16 at the other. Circle the division where 15.5 would be. Where would 15.65 go on your number line? How do you know? If you needed to round 15.65 to the nearest whole number, what number would that be? How do you know?*

5. Repeat for different numbers with two decimal places that come between 15 and 16.

Key checks: Do pupils understand that rounding decimal numbers is the same process as rounding whole numbers?

Extension: Ask pupils to make up numbers with two decimal places to give to a partner to round.

Support: Focus on rounding numbers with one decimal place only.

And again!

Strand: Number – fractions (including decimals and percentages)

Learning objective: To round decimals with two decimal places to one decimal place.

You will need: laminated empty number lines with 10 division

1. **Ask:** *How do we round a number with one decimal place to the nearest whole number? Can you explain in a different way? How would we know when to round up?* (if the number is 0.5 or more) *How would we know when to round down?* (if the number is less than 0.5) *What do you think it means to round a number to one decimal place?* (it is exactly the same as rounding to a whole number) *What can you tell me about 8.27?* (the digit 8 is in the ones and is multiplied by one to get its true value, 2 is in the tenths position and is multiplied by one tenth, 7 is in the hundredths position and is multiplied by one hundredth) *How do you think we would round 8.27 to one decimal place?* (round up because the digit in the hundredths position is more than 5) *What is 8.27 rounded to one decimal place?* (8.3) *What about 8.71?* (8.7)

2. Call out different numbers (e.g. 8.33, 8.39, 8.35). Pupils put their thumbs up if the number needs rounding up or their thumbs down if the number needs rounding down.

3. **Say:** *Write 8.5 at one end of an empty number line and 8.6 at the other. Circle the division where 8.55 would be. Which numbers would be rounded up to 8.6? How do you know? Which numbers would be rounded down to 8.5? How do you know?*

4. **Ask:** *Where would 8.58 go on your number line? How do you know? If you needed to round 8.58 to the nearest decimal place, what number would that be?*

5. Repeat for different numbers with two decimal places that come between 8.5 and 8.6.

Key checks: Do pupils understand that rounding to one decimal place is the same process as rounding to the nearest whole number?

Extension: Ask pupils to make up numbers with two decimal places to give to a partner to round to one decimal place.

Support: Focus on rounding to one decimal place using a number line.

Problems, problems

Strand: Number – fractions (including decimals and percentages)

Learning objective: To solve number problems and practical problems that involve rounding.

You will need: notes and coins, catalogue pages

1. **Ask:** *Why is it helpful to round numbers?* (e.g. if we need an approximate answer) *What can you tell me about the digits in £5.98?* (5 is in the ones position and is multiplied by one to give its true value of £5, 9 is in the tenths position and is multiplied by one tenth to give its value of nine tenths of a pound, and 8 is in the hundredths position and is multiplied by one hundredth to give its value of eight hundredths of a pound) *What is the same about this amount of money and the number 5.98?* (its value) *What is different?* (it is an amount of money) *How would we round £5.98 to the nearest pound?* (round up to £6) *How would we round £5.26 to the nearest pound?* (round down to £5)

2. Call out different amounts of money (e.g. £12.65, £12.24, £12.50). Pupils put their thumbs up if the amount needs rounding up to the next pound or their thumbs down if the amount needs rounding down.

3. Give pupils a selection of notes and coins. Ask them to make different amounts using the fewest notes and coins possible (e.g. £5.15, £7.36, £10.85). Once they have made each amount, they round it to the nearest pound, explaining how they knew whether to round up or down.

4. **Say:** *Elsa had £20. She wanted to buy a book which cost £8.99 and a colouring set for £12.25. How can you work out approximately what the total cost of the book and colouring set is?* (round the prices to the nearest whole pound) *What are the rounded prices?* (£9 and £12) *Does Elsa have enough money?*

5. Repeat for similar problems within the context of money.

Key checks: Can pupils make amounts of money using the fewest notes and coins? Do they understand that rounding for money is the same as rounding other numbers?

Extension: Ask pupils to choose pairs of items to buy from a catalogue. They round the prices to see approximately how much money they need.

Support: Focus on making amounts of money using fewest notes and coins and then rounding to the nearest pound.

More problems

Strand: Number – fractions (including decimals and percentages)

Learning objective: To solve problems involving number up to three decimal places.

You will need: digital weighing scales that give readings to three decimal places

1. **Ask:** *What can you tell me about the digits in 2.825?* (2 is in the ones and is multiplied by one to give its true value of 2, 8 is in the tenths and is multiplied by one tenth to give its true value of eight tenths and so on.) *How is 2.825 the same as 2.825kg?* (the digits have the same values) *How are they different?* (One is a number and the other is a mass.) *How would we round 2.825kg to the nearest kilogram?* (The mass is higher than 2.5kg so it would be rounded up to 3kg.)

2. Call out different masses (e.g. 5.257kg, 5.945kg, 5.725kg). Pupils put their thumbs up if the amount needs rounding up to the next kilogram or their thumbs down if the amount needs rounding down.

3. Give groups a set of digital scales. **Say:** *We are going to weigh different items from around the classroom. You need to record the masses and then round them to the nearest kilogram.* **Ask:** *Can you explain how you know whether to round up or down?*

4. **Ask:** *The vet weighed Freddie's two kittens. One weighed 1.357kg and the other weighed 1.578kg. What was their total mass to the nearest kilogram? How do you know?* (round 1.375kg to 1kg and 1.578kg to 2kg, giving an approximate mass of 3kg)

5. Repeat for similar problems within the context of mass.

Key checks: Do pupils use the word weight to describe how heavy something is? The correct word is mass. Do they understand that rounding for mass is the same as rounding other numbers?

Extension: Ask pupils to make up their own similar problems to give to a partner to solve.

Support: Focus on reading scales. Pupils continue to find the mass of different items and round these to the nearest kilogram.

The Romans

Strand: Number – number and place value

Learning objective: To read Roman numerals to 1000 (M) and recognise years written in Roman numerals.

You will need: a copy of this table per pupil:

Ones	I	II	III	IV	V	VI	VII	VIII	IX
Tens	X	XX	XXX	XL	L	LX	LXX	LXXX	XC
Hundreds	C	CC	CCC	CD	D	DC	DCC	DCCC	CM

1. **Ask:** *What can you tell me about Roman numerals?* (e.g. They were developed by the Romans thousands of years ago, they are not commonly used anymore, numbers were represented by letters.) *Where have you seen Roman numerals? Anywhere else?* (e.g. dates of film productions, clocks, introductory pages of a book)

2. Give each pupil a copy of the numeral table. **Ask:** *Can you see a pattern in the numerals? Can you explain that pattern? Can you explain any others? What do you think V stands for?* (5) *Why?* (it's the fifth value) *Why do you think four is IV?* (one before five) *Why do you think six is VI?* (one after five) Continue asking questions about other representations in each row.

3. **Ask:** *How do you think the Romans would have written 14? Can you explain why?* (XIV because X = 10 and IV = 4) *What about 57? Can you explain why?* (LVII because L = 50 and VII = 7) *What do you notice about the way the Romans made their numbers?* (They made them like we make ours; tens first then ones.)

4. Give pupils two-digit numbers to write as Roman numerals. Repeat for three-digit numbers.

5. Write numbers in Roman numerals for pupils to change to our numbers. Model this example:
CCCXLVI = CCC + XL + V + I = 300 + 40 (10 before 50) + 5 + 1 = 346

Key checks: Can pupils see the pattern in Roman numerals? Can pupils translate Roman numerals into our numbers?

Extension: The Romans used M for 1000 and MM for 2000 (e.g. MCDLXIV = M + CD + L + X + IV = 1000 + 400 (100 before 500) + 50 + 10 + 4 = 1464). Ask pupils to write today's date in Roman numerals.

Support: Focus on changing our two-digit numbers to Roman numerals and vice versa.

Turning decimals to fractions

Strand: Number – fractions (including decimals and percentages)

Learning objective: To read and write decimal numbers as fractions (for example, 0.71 = $\frac{71}{100}$).

You will need: place value grids that include tenths and hundredths, digit cards, whiteboard, whiteboard pen

1. Ask pupils to use their digit cards to make 7.4 on their place value grids. **Ask:** *What can you tell me about 7.4? Is there anything else?* (Seven is in the ones position and is multiplied by one to give its true value of seven, four is in the tenths position and is multiplied by one tenth to give its true value of four tenths, the two values are added together to give the whole number.) *How else can we say 7.4? Can you explain why?* (7.4 is equivalent to 7 and four tenths.) Repeat for other one-digit numbers with one decimal place.

2. **Ask:** *How can we write 0.4 as a fraction?* ($\frac{4}{10}$) *Can you explain why? Can you write 0.7 as a fraction on the board?* ($\frac{7}{10}$) Repeat for other tenths.

3. Ask pupils to use their digit cards to make 7.45 on their place value grids. **Ask:** *What can you tell me about the digit 5 in 7.45? Is there anything else?* (5 is positioned in the hundredths and multiplied by one hundredth to give the value of five hundredths.) *How can we show 0.4 as hundredths? Can you explain why?* (0.4 is equivalent to forty hundredths.) Repeat for other one-digit numbers with two decimal places.

4. Write a few tenths on the board as decimals. Pupils write them as tenths and hundredths in fractions, e.g. 0.6 ($\frac{6}{10}$, $\frac{60}{100}$), 0.5 ($\frac{5}{10}$, $\frac{50}{100}$), 0.9 ($\frac{9}{10}$, $\frac{90}{100}$).

5. Write a few hundredths on the board as decimals. Pupils write them as hundredths, e.g. 0.15 ($\frac{15}{100}$), 0.84 ($\frac{84}{100}$), 0.43 ($\frac{43}{100}$).

Key checks: Do pupils understand the link between decimals and fractions?

Extension: Pupils make up different single-digit numbers with two decimal places and write these as mixed numbers (e.g. 3.25 = $3\frac{25}{100}$).

Support: Focus on converting decimal tenths to fractions.

Equivalences

Strand: Number – fractions (including decimals and percentages)

Learning objective: To identify, name and write equivalent fractions of a given fraction, represented visually, including tenths and hundredths.

You will need: strips of paper, whiteboard, whiteboard pen

1. **Say:** *Take four strips of paper. Keep the first strip whole and label it 1. Take a second strip and fold it in half and label each part $\frac{1}{2}$. Fold the third strip in half and half again and label each part $\frac{1}{4}$. Fold the last strip in half, in half again and in half a third time and label each part $\frac{1}{8}$.*

2. **Ask:** *How many halves are equivalent to one whole?* Guide pupils to work out that two halves are equivalent to one whole. **Ask:** *What about quarters? Eighths? How many quarters are equivalent to one half?* Together, say the equivalence statement. **Ask:** *What about eighths? How many eighths are equivalent to one quarter?* Together, say the equivalence statement.

3. **Say:** *Take another three strips of paper. Fold one strip into thirds and label. Fold a second strip into thirds and then in half and label each part $\frac{1}{6}$. Fold the third strip into thirds and then halve and halve again and label each part $\frac{1}{12}$.*

4. **Ask:** *What equivalences can you see? What others? How many sixths are equivalent to one third? How many are equivalent to one half?* Explore all other equivalences (e.g. $\frac{2}{3} = \frac{4}{6}$).

5. Together, write all the equivalences found on the board. **Say:** *Look at the numerators and denominators in $\frac{1}{2}$ and $\frac{2}{4}$. What could we do to the numerator and denominator in $\frac{1}{2}$ to make $\frac{2}{4}$?* (multiply by 2) *What could you do to the numerator and denominator in $\frac{1}{2}$ to make $\frac{4}{8}$? $\frac{3}{6}$? $\frac{6}{12}$?* (multiply by 4, 3 and 6 respectively) *What could you do to the numerator and denominator in $\frac{6}{12}$ to make $\frac{1}{2}$?* (divide by 6)

6. Repeat for the other equivalences. **Ask:** *What generalisation can we make?* (You need to multiply or divide the numerator and denominator by the same number to find equivalent fractions.)

Key checks: Do pupils understand how to use the generalisation to find equivalent fractions?

Extension: Pupils make lists of other equivalent fractions including tenths and hundredths using the generalisation.

Support: Measure and make fraction strips for fifths and tenths. Pupils explore equivalences with these (e.g. $\frac{2}{5} = \frac{4}{10}$).

Comparing fractions

Strand: Number – fractions (including decimals and percentages)

Learning objective: To compare and order fractions whose denominators are all multiples of the same number.

You will need: strips of paper

1. **Say:** *Take four strips of paper. Keep the first strip whole and label it 1. Take a second strip and fold it in half and label each part $\frac{1}{2}$. Fold the third strip in half and half again, and label each part $\frac{1}{4}$. Then fold the last strip in half, in half again and in half a third time and label each part $\frac{1}{8}$.*

2. **Ask:** *What can you tell me about your strips of paper? What fractions have you made? How many halves are equivalent to one whole? What about quarters? Eighths? Can you see any other equivalences?*

3. **Ask:** *Look at one half and one quarter. Which is the greater fraction? Can you explain why? What about one half and one eighth? Can you explain why? What about one quarter and one eighth? Can you explain why?*

4. Ask pupils to use their fraction strips. **Ask:** *Which is greater $\frac{3}{8}$ or $\frac{1}{4}$?* ($\frac{1}{4}$ is equivalent to $\frac{2}{8}$ which is smaller than $\frac{3}{8}$) *How do you know?* Repeat for other eighths, quarters and halves. (e.g. *Which is the smallest fraction, $\frac{7}{8}$ or $\frac{1}{2}$, $\frac{3}{4}$ or $\frac{1}{2}$?*) Ask pupils to explain their thinking.

5. Repeat the whole process by making fraction strips for thirds, sixths and twelfths.

6. Give pupils three different fractions from each set of strips and ask them to order these from least to greatest (e.g. $\frac{1}{2}$, $\frac{3}{4}$ and $\frac{5}{8}$ / $\frac{2}{3}$, $\frac{5}{6}$ and $\frac{7}{12}$). Expect them to compare the strips and also compare by changing the fractions to the same denominator (e.g. $\frac{4}{8}$, $\frac{6}{8}$, $\frac{5}{8}$ and $\frac{8}{12}$, $\frac{10}{12}$, $\frac{7}{12}$).

Key checks: Are pupils making the mistake of looking at the denominator and comparing fractions according to the size of that number as a whole digit? For example, do they think $\frac{1}{8}$ is greater than $\frac{1}{2}$ because 8 is greater than 2? Can pupils change the fractions to the same denominator?

Extension: Pupils order sets of four fractions without using their strips of paper.

Support: Focus on comparing two fractions.

Mix them up

Strand: Number – fractions (including decimals and percentages)

Learning objective: To recognise mixed numbers and improper fractions and convert from one form to the other and write mathematical statements > 1 as a mixed number [for example, $\frac{2}{5} + \frac{4}{5} = \frac{6}{5} = 1\frac{1}{5}$].

You will need: strips of paper, scissors

1. **Say:** *Take two strips of paper and fold them into halves.* **Ask:** *How many whole strips of paper do you have?* (two) *How many halves is that?* (four) Write '$2 = \frac{4}{2}$'. **Say:** *Cut the strips to make them into halves and put three side by side.* **Ask:** *How many halves do you have now? How else can we describe three halves?* Write '$\frac{3}{2} = 1\frac{1}{2}$'.

2. **Say:** *$\frac{3}{2}$ is called an improper fraction.* **Ask:** *Why do you think this is called an improper fraction? What generalisation do you think we can develop about improper fractions?* (The numerator is greater than the denominator.) **Say:** *$1\frac{1}{2}$ is called a mixed number.* **Ask:** *Why do you think this is called a mixed number? What generalisation do you think we can develop about mixed numbers?* (A mixed number is made from a whole number and a fraction.) **Ask:** *How are $\frac{3}{2}$ and $1\frac{1}{2}$ the same? How are they different?* Guide pupils to work out that they have the same value but different representation.

3. Repeat using strips of paper for quarters.

4. **Say:** *Place two quarters and three quarters side by side.* **Ask:** *How many quarters are there altogether?* (five quarters) *What is that as a mixed number?* ($1\frac{1}{4}$) *How could we describe this using an addition statement?* ($\frac{2}{4} + \frac{3}{4} = \frac{5}{4} = 1\frac{1}{4}$)

5. Repeat for thirds and sixths.

Key checks: Do pupils understand that an improper fraction and its equivalent mixed number are a different representation of the same value?

Extension: Ask pupils to work out the generalisation that can be made for changing an improper fraction to a mixed number. Can they reason that they divide the numerator by the denominator to make a mixed number? For example $\frac{5}{3}$: divide 5 by 3 to give one whole and $\frac{2}{3}$.

Support: Measure and make fraction strips for fifths. Pupils use these to explore improper fractions and mixed numbers with fifths.

Add and subtract

Strand: Number – fractions (including decimals and percentages)

Learning objective: To add and subtract fractions with the same denominator and denominators that are multiples of the same number.

You will need: strips of paper, scissors, whiteboard, whiteboard pen

1. Ask pupils to use strips of paper. They keep one strip whole and fold three strips to show halves, quarters and eighths. They then cut up the fractions.

2. **Ask:** *Can you make one whole using a mixture of fractions?* Ask them to move the fraction parts, so they mix them and line them up under the whole strip. **Ask:** *Can you explain what you have done? How many different ways can you find?* Pupils record their additions (e.g. $\frac{1}{2} + \frac{2}{4} = 1$, $\frac{1}{2} + \frac{1}{4} + \frac{2}{8} = 1$).

3. **Ask:** *Can you take a fraction away from one whole? What subtraction have you made? Can you make a different one? And another?* Pupils record their subtractions (e.g. $1 - \frac{7}{8} = \frac{1}{8}$, $1 - \frac{1}{4} = \frac{3}{4}$).

4. **Ask:** *How could we add $\frac{1}{2}$ and $\frac{3}{8}$ without using fraction strips?* (make them into equivalent fractions) *How many eighths are equivalent to one half? What addition statement can we make?* Invite a pupil to write it on the board: $\frac{1}{2} + \frac{3}{8} = \frac{4}{8} + \frac{3}{8} = \frac{7}{8}$.

5. **Ask:** *How could we subtract $\frac{1}{4}$ from $\frac{7}{8}$?* (make them into equivalent fractions) *How many eighths are equivalent to one quarter? What subtraction statement can we make?* Invite a pupil to write it on the board: $\frac{7}{8} - \frac{2}{8} = \frac{5}{8}$.

6. Repeat for thirds, sixths and twelfths.

Key checks: Can pupils use their understanding of equivalence to add and subtract fractions?

Extension: Give pupils different fractions that are multiples of the same number to add and subtract. For example, fifths and tenths. They record the additions and subtractions they make, changing any improper fractions to mixed numbers (e.g. $\frac{3}{5} + \frac{7}{10} = \frac{6}{10} + \frac{7}{10} = \frac{13}{10} = 1\frac{3}{10}$).

Support: Focus on adding and subtracting halves, quarters and eighths.

Multiply

Strand: Number – fractions (including decimals and percentages)

Learning objective: To multiply proper fractions and mixed numbers by whole numbers, supported by materials and diagrams.

You will need: strips of paper, scissors, whiteboard, whiteboard pen

1. **Ask:** *What can you tell me about multiplication? What else?* (e.g. multiplication is repeated addition, grouping, inverse of division) *What does $\frac{1}{2} \times 5$ mean?* (5 groups of one half, $\frac{1}{2} + \frac{1}{2} + \frac{1}{2} + \frac{1}{2} + \frac{1}{2}$)

2. Give pupils strips of paper. They fold each in half and cut them. **Say:** *Place five halves in a line.* **Ask:** *How many halves do you have? How many wholes is that? Do you have any halves left? What is $\frac{1}{2} \times 5$?* ($\frac{1}{2} \times 5 = \frac{5}{2} = 2\frac{1}{2}$) Write $\frac{1}{2} \times 5 = \frac{5}{2}$ on the board. Repeat for other numbers of halves.

3. **Ask:** *How could we multiply one and a half by five? What do we already know?* ($\frac{1}{2} \times 5 = \frac{5}{2} = 2\frac{1}{2}$) *What do we need to do now?* (add the product of 1×5) *What is $1\frac{1}{2} \times 5$?* ($5 + 2\frac{1}{2} = 7\frac{1}{2}$) *If we know that $1\frac{1}{2} \times 5 = 7\frac{1}{2}$, what else do we know?* ($5 \times 1\frac{1}{2} = 7\frac{1}{2}$, $7\frac{1}{2} \div 5 = 1\frac{1}{2}$, $7\frac{1}{2} \div 1\frac{1}{2} = 5$)

4. Pupils fold more strips of paper to make quarters and cut these. **Ask:** *How could we use these strips to find the product of $\frac{3}{4}$ and three?* Pupils lay three quarters on the table. They do this three times, placing the parts side by side. **Ask:** *How many quarters are there altogether?* (9) Write $\frac{3}{4} \times 3 = \frac{9}{4}$ on the board beside $\frac{1}{2} \times 5 = \frac{5}{2}$ and the other halves you multiplied. **Ask:** *What is $\frac{9}{4}$ as a mixed number?* ($2\frac{1}{4}$) *How do you know? If we know that $\frac{3}{4} \times 3 = 2\frac{1}{4}$, what else do we know?*

5. Repeat for $1\frac{3}{4} \times 3$ and then for other numbers of quarters.

Key checks: Can pupils link multiplication to repeated addition?

Extension: Ask pupils to look at the multiplication statements you wrote on the board and to work out the generalisation for multiplying fractions by whole numbers (multiply the numerator and multiplier together).

Support: Focus on multiplying unit fractions.

Percentages

Strand: Number – fractions (including decimals and percentages)

Learning objective: To recognise the per cent symbol (%) and understand that per cent relates to 'the number of parts per hundred', and to write percentages as a fraction with the denominator 100, and as a decimal.

You will need: 10 × 10 square pieces of paper, place value grid for demonstration, digit cards: 1 and two zeros, whiteboard, whiteboard pen

1. Give pupils pieces of squared paper. **Ask:** *What can you tell me about your squared paper?* (e.g. 10 × 10 array of 100 squares) *If the whole square is one whole, what is each small square? Can you explain how you know?* Demonstrate dividing one by 100 on the place value grid: divide one by 10 to give one tenth and then by 10 again to give one hundredth. **Ask:** *How else can we say one hundredth?* (0.01) *What would five squares be? Can you tell me as a fraction and a decimal?* ($\frac{5}{100}$ and 0.05) *What about 10 squares?* ($\frac{10}{100}$, $\frac{1}{10}$, 0.1)

2. Ask pupils to shade different fractions and record them and their equivalent decimal.

3. Write the percentage symbol on the board. **Ask:** *Where have you seen this in real life?* (e.g. sales in shop windows, clothes labels, food packaging) *Can you explain what it tells us?* (e.g. in a sale, the part of the whole cost that has been taken away, in clothes the part of the whole which is made of a particular fabric) **Say:** *A percentage is another type of fraction. It is part of a whole. This whole is always split into 100 parts.*

4. **Ask:** *If the whole of your square paper represents 100%, what would one square be? What would five squares be? What do you notice?* (Percentages are the same value as hundredths.)

5. Ask pupils to add the equivalent percentages to the fractions and decimals they recorded in step 2.

Key checks: Can pupils make the links between fractions, decimals and percentages?

Extension: Ask pupils to make a list of different hundredths as fractions and then the equivalent decimals and percentages.

Support: Focus on tenths and the equivalent decimals and percentages.

Yet more problems

Strand: Number – fractions (including decimals and percentages)

Learning objective: To solve problems which require knowing percentage and decimal equivalents of $\frac{1}{2}$, $\frac{1}{4}$, $\frac{1}{5}$, $\frac{2}{5}$, $\frac{4}{5}$ and those fractions with a denominator of a multiple of 10 or 25.

You will need: 10 × 10 square pieces of paper, coloured pencils

1. Give pupils pieces of squared paper. **Say:** *The square paper represents one whole. Shade 20 squares. What fraction of the whole is shaded? What is that as a decimal? What is that as a percentage? Can you explain how you know? What fraction of the whole is not shaded? What is that as a decimal? What is that as a percentage? Can you explain how you know?* Repeat with other percentages.

2. **Ask:** *If the whole of your square paper represents £100, how much would 20 squares be worth? What about 50 squares? 25 squares? If it is worth £200, what would 20 squares be worth? 50 squares? 25 squares?*

3. **Ask:** *If a whole value is £180, what is 10%? How would you work that out?* (divide £180 by 10 = £18) *How could you use your answer to 10% of £180 to work out 5% of £180?* (halve £18) *What is 5% of £180? How could you use 10% to work out 20%?* (double £18) *What is 20% of £180? How could you use this information to find 15%?* (add 10% and 5%) *How can you use it to find 30%?* (add 20% and 10%) Ask pupils to write down as many percentages as they can of £180 by doubling, halving, adding and subtracting.

4. **Say:** *In a sale there is a 10% reduction on books. If the books cost £20 before the sale, how much are they in the sale? What if there was a 5% reduction? What if there was a 20% reduction?*

Key checks: Can pupils make percentages of amounts using amounts they have already found?

Extension: Ask pupils to find as many percentages as they can if the whole is £240.

Support: Ask pupils to find 10% of £200 and then to use this to make 5%, 20%, 25% and so on.

Addition and subtraction

Strand: Number – addition and subtraction

Learning objective: To add and subtract whole numbers with more than four digits, including using formal written methods (columnar addition and subtraction).

You will need: coloured counters (red = 1000, blue = 100, green = 10, orange = 1), whiteboard, whiteboard pen

1. **Say:** *Make 2345 and 1827 using coloured counters.* **Ask:** *How can we use the counters to demonstrate the addition of these two numbers?* Ask pupils to combine the ones. *How many ones are there? Why can't we leave 12 ones in the ones position?* (12 is equivalent to 10 and 2, so there is a ten.) *Can you explain what we need to do?* Pupils exchange 10 ones for a ten. They then combine the tens. *How many tens are there altogether?* (7) Next they combine the hundreds. *How many hundreds are there? Why can't we leave 11 hundreds in the hundreds position?* (11 hundreds is equivalent to 1000 and 100, so there is a thousand.) *Can you explain what we need to do?* Pupils exchange 10 hundreds for a thousand. They then combine the thousands.

2. **Ask:** *How can we show what we did with the counters as a written method?* Pupils repeat the calculation practically as you model the written method.

3. **Ask:** *How can we check that our answer is correct? How else?* (e.g. add the numbers in a different order, use the inverse) *How can we check using the inverse?* Ask pupils to subtract 1827 from 4172. **Ask:** *Can we subtract seven from two? What do we need to do?* Pupils exchange a ten for 10 ones, add to the two and then subtract seven. As they do this, you model the written method. **Ask:** *What do we need to do next? How can you do this with your counters? How can I show this in my written method?* Continue in this way until you have 2345.

4. Repeat for other four-digit numbers. Ensure that exchanges are required.

Key checks: Do pupils understand how to check an answer using the inverse? Do they understand the concept of exchange for addition and subtraction?

Extension: Ask pupils to use digit cards to generate pairs of four-digit numbers to add and check using subtraction.

Support: Give pupils four-digit numbers that have an exchange in the ones only.

Sequencing

Strand: Number – addition and subtraction

Learning objective: To add numbers mentally with increasingly large numbers.

You will need: coloured counters (red = 1000, blue = 100, green = 10, orange = 1), whiteboard, whiteboard pen

1. **Say:** *Make 3142 and 1326 using coloured counters. Now combine your counters.* **Ask:** *What is the sum of these two numbers?* (4468) *Do we need to use a written method for this calculation or can we use a mental calculation strategy?* (pupils should feel confident completing this mentally) *Why do you think that?* (because no exchanges are needed) *Can you think of a method that we could use?*

2. Explain that sequencing would be a good strategy. Pupils keep one number whole and partition the second one. Model on the board: 3142 + 1000 + 300 + 20 + 6.

3. **Ask:** *If we know that 3142 + 1326 = 4468, what else do we know? Why?* (1326 + 3142 = 4468 because addition is commutative, 4468 – 3142 = 1326 and 4468 – 1326 = 3142 because subtraction is the inverse of addition.)

4. Ask pupils to find the sums of 2314 and 2163, and 4426 and 3273. They do this by making the numbers using counters and adding the thousands, then the hundreds, tens and ones. They record as you have demonstrated. They then write the associated commutative and inverse facts.

5. **Ask:** *Can we use sequencing to add 23.24 and 21.34? Why?* (yes, because there is no exchange needed) *What is 23.24 add 20? What is 43.24 add 1? What is 44.24 add three tenths? What is 44.54 add four hundredths?*

6. Repeat for other numbers with two decimal places.

7. **Ask:** *What should we do when we are asked to add two numbers together?* (Check to see if we can use a mental calculations strategy.) *Can you explain why?* (e.g. it is quicker and more efficient)

Key checks: Do pupils understand the method of sequencing for addition?

Extension: Ask pupils to make up their own calculations that can be added using sequencing.

Support: Add three-digit numbers using sequencing.

More sequencing

Strand: Number – addition and subtraction

Learning objective: To subtract numbers mentally with increasingly large numbers.

You will need: coloured counters (red = 1000, blue = 100, green = 10, orange = 1)

1. **Say:** *The baker baked 3764 rolls. He sold 1652 in the morning. He sold the rest in the afternoon. How many did he sell in the afternoon? What do we need to find out? How can we do this? What do we need to do to solve the problem?* (subtract 1652 from 3764) *How do you know?* (clues in the problem)

2. Get pupils to make 3764 using coloured counters. **Ask:** *Is it necessary to use a written method for this calculation or can we use a mental calculation strategy?* (Pupils should feel confident completing this mentally.) *Why do you think that?* (because no exchanges are needed) *Can you think of a method that we could use?*

3. Explain that sequencing is a good strategy for subtraction as well as addition, if the numbers work. Ask pupils to take away one thousand from their counters, then six hundreds, five tens and two ones. As they do, model the recording on the board: 3764 – 1000 – 600 – 50 – 2. Agree that the baker sold 2112 rolls in the afternoon.

4. **Ask:** *How can we check to make sure we are correct? Why?* (Add the two smaller numbers to see if we have the number of rolls the baker baked because addition is the inverse of subtraction.) Pupils do this using sequencing.

5. Ask the problem again, but change the number of rolls that he sold in the morning to 2131 and then 1523. Pupils make 3764 using counters and subtract the thousands, then the hundreds, tens and ones. They record as you have demonstrated. They then check by adding the two smaller numbers.

6. **Ask:** *What should we do when we are asked to subtract one number from another?* (Check to see if a mental calculations strategy would be quicker and more efficient.)

Key checks: Do pupils understand the method of sequencing for subtraction?

Extension: Ask pupils to make up problems for a partner to solve using sequencing.

Support: Subtract three-digit numbers using sequencing.

Rounding and adjusting

Strand: Number – addition and subtraction

Learning objective: To add and subtract numbers mentally with increasingly large numbers.

You will need: coloured counters (red = 1000, blue = 100, green = 10, orange = 1), whiteboard, whiteboard pen

1. **Say:** *Samir scored 2567 points on a computer game. Frankie scored 1999 points more. How many points did Frankie score? What do we need to find out? How can we do this? What do we need to do to solve the problem?* (add 2567 and 1999) *How do you know?* (clues in the problem)

2. Ask pupils to make 2567 using coloured counters. **Ask:** *Is it necessary to use a written method for this calculation or can we use a mental calculation strategy?* (Pupils should feel confident completing this mentally.) *Can you think of a method that we could use?* Explain that rounding and adjusting is a good strategy for addition when numbers are a near multiple of 10/100/1000. **Ask:** *What multiple of 1000 is 1999 closest to? How should we adjust? Can you explain why?* (Subtract one because 2000 is one more than 1999.) Ask pupils to add two thousands to 2567 and then subtract one. As they do, model the recording on the board: 2567 + 2000 – 1. Agree that Frankie scored 4566 points.

3. **Ask:** *How can we check to make sure we are correct?* (Subtract 1999 from 4566 because subtraction is the inverse of addition.) Pupils do this by rounding and adjusting. **Ask:** *How would we round and adjust this time? Why?* (Subtract 2000 and add one because we have taken one too many away.)

4. Ask the problem again but change the number of points scored by Samir to 1356 and then 3782. Pupils make Samir's points using counters and add two thousand and subtract one. They record as you have demonstrated. They then check by subtracting 2000 from Frankie's score and adding one.

Key checks: Can pupils understand the method of rounding and adjusting for addition?

Extension: Ask pupils to make up problems for a partner to solve using rounding and adjusting.

Support: Add three-digit numbers using rounding and adjusting.

Counting on

Strand: Number – addition and subtraction

Learning objective: To add and subtract mentally with increasingly large numbers.

You will need: coloured rods or strips of paper (scissors if using paper)

1. **Say:** *Shelley had 345 shells, Beth had 278 shells.* **Ask:** *How many more shells did Shelley have? What is the key word in the question?* (the word more) *Do we need to add or subtract to find the solution?* (Either, we need to find the difference so we can add to count on or subtract to count back.)

2. Help pupils to use the bar model to represent the problem. Use coloured rods or strips of paper to make a representation of the problem: one longer rod/strip to represent 345 and two others (one representing 278) that together are the same length as the longer one (345):

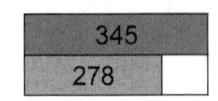

3. **Ask:** *If the longest rod/strip represents Shelley's 345 shells and one of the others represents Beth's 278 shells, how can we find the other part or the difference between the two amounts?* (count back from 345 to 278 or count on from 278 to 345) Together, do both. **Ask:** *Which is easiest? Why?*

4. Ask the problem several more times, varying it slightly. Keep Shelley's shells the same and vary the number Beth has to 178, 275, 265. **Ask:** *What is the same about this problem? What is different? Can you see any patterns?*

5. **Say:** *Toby had 745 football cards. Hassid had 634. How many did they have altogether? What is the key word in the question?* (altogether) *How can we solve this problem? Do we need to add or subtract?* (add) *How do you know?* (clue in the problem: altogether)

6. Use a bar model to represent the problem. **Say:** *The two top bars represent 745 and 634, the bottom bar represents the whole.* **Ask:** *Can you use sequencing to count on?*

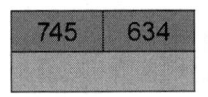

7. Ask the problem again, but vary the amount of cards Hassid has.

Key checks: Do pupils understand counting on for subtraction? Do they know how to use the bar model to represent problems?

Extension: Ask pupils to make up problems for a partner to solve.

Support: Focus on the use of the bar model.

Problems with money

Strand: Number – addition and subtraction, Measurement

Learning objective: To solve addition and subtraction multi-step problems in contexts, deciding which operations and methods to use and why.

You will need: coins and notes (real, if possible), whiteboards, whiteboard pens

1. Give pupils a collection of coins and notes. Hold each coin and note up and ask pupils to tell you how many pence each is worth. **Ask:** *How can we make £12.83 using the smallest number of coins? What if we didn't have a 50p coin?* Repeat with other amounts.

2. **Say:** *Suzie is saving up to buy a bike. The bike she wants costs £250. Suzie has £165.50.* **Ask:** *How much more does she need to save? How can we work out the answer? Is there any other way?* Ask pupils to represent the problem using the bar model:

£250	
£165.50	

3. **Ask:** *How can we use this representation to help us?* (count on from £165.50 to £250 or count back from £250 to £165.50) Together, do both and discuss which is easier.

4. Ask the problem several more times, varying the amount Suzie has saved to £155.50, £145.50 and £135.50. **Ask:** *How is the problem the same? How is it different? What do you notice about the amounts that Suzie has saved?* (The tens digit decreases by one in each amount.)

5. **Say:** *Suzie has found out that the bike has been reduced by 20% in a sale.* **Ask:** *How much does she need to save now? How can we find 20% of £250?* (find 10% and double) *What is 20%?* (£50) *What do we need to do when we have found 20% of £250?* (subtract £50 from £250)

6. **Say:** *Draw a bar model to work out how much more Suzie needs to save to buy the bike at the new discounted price using her original savings of £165.50, and then how much she still needs based on the variations of her savings: £155.50, £145.50 and £135.50.*

Key check: Do pupils recognise coins and notes and know their values?

Extension: Pupils make up their own problems that involve both addition and subtraction of money for a partner to solve.

Support: Work with pupils who don't have a good understanding of coins and notes and their values. Ask them to make different amounts of money using the fewest notes and coins.

Problems with length

Strand: Number – addition and subtraction, Measurement

Learning objective: To solve addition and subtraction multi-step problems in contexts, deciding which operations and methods to use and why.

You will need: a world map, whiteboard, whiteboard pen

1. **Ask:** *How many metres are equivalent to one kilometre? What about 10 kilometres? Can you explain how you worked that out?* Repeat for other numbers of kilometres.

2. **Ask:** *What can you tell me about 1.275km?* (1km 275m, 275m = $\frac{275}{1000}$ of a kilometre, 1275m) *What about 1.5km? 2.125km?* Repeat for other kilometre lengths with decimals.

3. Write '3.258km' and '2.999km' on the board. **Ask:** *How can we find the total of the two lengths?* **Say:** *The two best methods would be rounding and adjusting (3.258km + 3km – 1m) or bridging 1 (take 1m from 3.258km and add to 2.999m to give 3.257km add 3km).* Use both methods to work out the total.

4. **Ask:** *How can we find the difference between these two lengths?* Focus on counting on from 2.999km. Model the calculation: add 0.001 to give 3km, then add 0.01 and 0.258 to give 0.259. **Ask:** *What is the difference between the two lengths?*

5. **Say:** *A pilot flew from London to Cairo, a distance of 3510km, and then from Cairo to Durban, a distance of 3088km. What was the total distance flown? Where are Cairo and Durban?* (pupils find the two cities on a map) *What information do we need to look at?* (the two distances) *What do we have to do to the numbers?* (add them) *Which strategy shall we use to add them?* Suggest sequencing. Invite a pupil to model how to do this.

6. **Ask:** *What is the difference between the two distances? Which strategy shall we use to find the difference?* Suggest rounding 3088km to 3100km, subtracting this from 3510km and then adding 12km back on. Together, work through the calculation.

7. Ask similar problems that involve using mental calculation strategies.

Key check: Can pupils use rounding and adjusting, bridging and sequencing to calculate mentally? Can they relate their work with tenths, hundredths and thousandths to length?

Extension: Pupils make up problems involving kilometres with up to three decimal places to give to a partner to solve.

Support: Focus on adding and subtracting kilometres such as 12.4km and 15.7km.

Problems with mass

Strand: Number – addition and subtraction, Measurement

Learning objective: To solve addition and subtraction multi-step problems in contexts, deciding which operations and methods to use and why.

You will need: digital weighing scales that show thousandths of a kilogram, objects to weigh from around the classroom

1. **Ask:** *What can you tell me about 3.245kg? What else?* (e.g. 3kg 245g, 3245g, 3.245 kg = 3 and $\frac{245}{1000}$ of a kilogram) *What is double that mass? Can you explain how you worked that out? What can you tell me about 6.49kg? What else?* (e.g. 6kg 490g, 6490g, 6.49kg = 6 and $\frac{49}{100}$ of a kilogram)

2. Ask groups of pupils to use the digital weighing scales to find the mass of two objects. They weigh these in whole kilograms and thousandths of a kilogram as appropriate. **Ask:** *How can you find the total mass of your two objects without weighing them together? What strategy could you use to add them?* Pupils choose a mental calculation strategy, if appropriate, and find the total mass. They then use a counting on method to find the difference in their masses.

3. **Say:** *An Asian elephant weighs about 5400kg. An African forest elephant weighs about 2700kg. What is their total mass? Which strategy shall we use to add them? Can you explain why?* Suggest bridging (take 300kg from 5400kg and add to 2700kg, giving 5100kg + 3000kg). **Ask:** *What is the difference in their masses? Which strategy shall we use?* (count on from 2700kg)

4. Ask similar problems that involve mental calculation strategies.

Key check: Do pupils choose appropriate mental calculation strategies? Can they accurately read digital weighing scales?

Extension: Pupils make up their own problems involving kilograms and grams. They give these to a partner to solve.

Support: Work with any pupils who have difficulty reading scales. Help them to practise weighing objects and reading the scale to the nearest 100g.

Problems with capacity

Strand: Number – addition and subtraction, Measurement

Learning objective: To solve addition and subtraction multi-step problems in contexts, deciding which operations and methods to use and why.

You will need: one measuring jug per group, 2L bottles of water, small containers

1. **Ask:** *What is meant by capacity?* (the amount a container can hold)
   Ask: *How many millilitres are equivalent to one litre? What about half a litre? Can you explain how you worked that out? What about quarter of a litre? How did you work that out?* Repeat for whole numbers of litres.

2. **Ask:** *What can you tell me about 2.5L? What else?* (e.g. 2L 500mL, $2\frac{1}{2}$L, 2500mL, 2.5L = 2 and $\frac{5}{10}$ of a litre) *What can you tell me about 3.25L?* (e.g. 3L 250mL, $3\frac{1}{4}$L, 3250mL, 3.25L = 3 and $\frac{25}{100}$ of a litre)

3. Give groups a container, some water and a measuring jug. Ask them to find the capacity of their container. Write all the capacities on the board. Order them from least to greatest capacity. Choose the least and the greatest.
   Ask: *How can we find their total capacity without using a measuring jug?* (add) *What strategy could we use to add them?* Help pupils to choose a mental calculation strategy or, if appropriate, the formal written method.
   Ask: *Can you explain how to carry out this strategy?* **Ask:** *What is the total?*

4. **Ask:** *How can we find the difference between these two capacities?* Focus on counting on. **Ask:** *What is the difference?*

5. **Ask:** *The capacity of a small pan is 0.9L and the capacity of a medium sized pan is 1.5L. What is the total capacity of the two pans? Can you explain your strategy for finding the total? What is the difference in their capacities? Can you explain your strategy for working out the difference?*

6. Ask other problems involving capacity.

Key check: Can pupils make the links between decimals in numbers and in measurements?

Extension: Pupils make up their own problems involving litres and millilitres in decimal format. They give these to a partner to solve.

Support: Focus on tenths, for example, 2.5L, 3.9L.

Problems with volume

Strand: Number – addition and subtraction, Measurement

Learning objective: To solve addition and subtraction multi-step problems in contexts, deciding which operations and methods to use and why.

You will need: one measuring jug per group, 2L bottles of water filled to different volumes, whiteboard, whiteboard pen

1. **Ask:** *What is meant by volume?* (the amount of liquid inside a container) *What units do we use to measure liquid volume?* (litres and millilitres)

2. Give groups a bottle of water and a measuring jug. Ask them to find the volume of water in the bottle. Write all the volumes on the board. Order them from least to greatest. Choose two volumes. **Ask:** *How can we find their total volume without using a measuring jug?* (add) *What strategy would you use to add them? Can you think of any others?* Help pupils to choose a mental calculation strategy or, if appropriate, the formal written method. *Can you explain how to carry out this strategy?* Pupils work out the total. **Ask:** *What is the total?*

3. **Ask:** *How can we find the difference between these two volumes?* Focus on counting on. Pupils work out the difference. **Ask:** *What is the difference?*

4. **Say:** *Adam has two containers of soup. One has a volume of 1.275L, the other has a volume of 2.125L. What is the total volume? What information do we need to look at? Which strategy shall we use?* Suggest looking for number bonds to 10 and 100. **Ask:** *What is the difference in their volumes? Which strategy shall we use to find the difference?* Suggest counting on.

5. Ask similar volume problems that involve number bonds to 10 and 100 for addition and counting on for finding the difference.

Key check: Do pupils understand the difference between capacity and volume?

Extension: Pupils make up their own volume problems involving litres and millilitres in decimal format. They give these to a partner to solve.

Support: Give volume problems to pupils to solve focusing on tenths, for example, 4.1L, 7.3L.

Problems with time

Strand: Number – addition and subtraction, Measurement

Learning objective: To solve addition and subtraction multi-step problems in contexts, deciding which operations and methods to use and why.

You will need: analogue clocks that pupils can manipulate or draw the times on, whiteboards, whiteboard pens

1. Give each pupil a clock. Call out a variety of times for them to show. For each, ask them to write down the equivalent 12-hour and 24-hour times. **Ask:** *What is the 12-hour digital time for 25 minutes to 3?* (2:35) *Can you explain why? How can we write 25 minutes to 3 as a 24-hour clock time?* (02:35 and 14:35) *Can you explain why?*

2. **Ask:** *How many minutes are there in an hour? What about two hours/four hours/eight hours? How did you work that out? Can you use this information to work out how many minutes in three hours/six hours/12 hours? Can you explain how you did that?*

3. **Ask:** *How can we find the difference in time between 07:35 and 14:20? Is there another way?* Draw a number line on the board with 07:35 at one end and 14:20 at the other. Count the minutes to 08:00, add the hours to 14:00 and then the remaining 20 minutes to give six hours and 45 minutes. *Could we have done this in a different way?* (counted on hours first and then the minutes from 13:35) Repeat for other time differences.

4. **Say:** *Sam went shopping. She left home at 08:30 and got back at 17:05. How long was she away from home? What information do we need to look at? What do we have to do?* Pupils solve the problem. **Ask:** *Can you explain how you worked out your answer?*

5. Ask similar problems that involve time durations.

Key check: Can pupils find times on clocks? Can they choose appropriate mental calculation strategies?

Extension: Pupils make up problems that involve finding time differences and durations. They give these to a partner to solve.

Support: Work with any pupils who have difficulty using 12-hour and 24-hour times. Draw a number line with the 12-hour clock hour times on the top and the equivalent 24-hour clock hour times underneath. Show analogue clock times and ask pupils to identify both 12-hour and 24-hour digital times.

Multiples and factors

Strand: Number – multiplication and division

Learning objective: To identify multiples and factors, including finding all factor pairs of a number, and common factors of two numbers.

You will need: digit cards, whiteboard, whiteboard pen

1. **Ask:** *What is a multiple?* (the product of two numbers) *Can you give an example? What is your multiple the product of? Can you give another example?* Write examples pupils give you on the board. Invite pupils to write the pairs of numbers that make the multiples underneath.

2. Give each pupil a set of digit cards. **Say:** *Shuffle the cards and place them face down on the table. Turn over the top card and write down as many multiples as you can in one minute.* **Ask:** *Can you give me some examples of your multiples?* Repeat two or three times.

3. **Ask:** *What is a factor?* (A number that is multiplied to give a product.) *What are the factors of 12?* (1, 2, 3, 4, 6, 12) *How do you know they are factors? Can you give another example of a factor? Explain how you know.*

4. Write 24 on the board. Ask pupils to find all of its factors. **Ask:** *How do you know you have all the factors?* (1, 2, 3, 4, 6, 8, 12, 24 because these are the only numbers that 24 is a multiple of)

5. **Ask:** *What do you think is meant by a factor pair?* (the two numbers which are multiplied together to give a product) Ask pupils to write down the factor pairs for 48 (1 and 48, 2 and 24, 3 and 16, 4 and 12, 6 and 8).

6. **Ask:** *What do you think is meant by a common factor?* (a factor that is the same for two numbers) *What are the common factors of 24 and 48?* (1, 2, 3, 4, 6, 8, 12, 24)

7. **Ask:** *Ignoring zero, can you think of a number that doesn't have any factors? Why do you think that isn't possible?* (all numbers are made up of the number and one) *Which number has the fewest factors?* (one)

Key check: Do pupils understand the key vocabulary of multiple, factor, factor pair and common factor?

Extension: Pupils make two-digit numbers using their digit cards. For each number, they find all the factor pairs and write them down. They do this three times and then circle all the common factors.

Support: Give pupils multiplication tables to help them identify multiples. For each one they write the two factors that make the multiple.

All about primes

Strand: Number – multiplication and division

Learning objective: To know and use the vocabulary of prime numbers, prime factors and composite (non-prime) numbers.

Note: It is important that pupils understand that one is a composite number. It only has one factor.

You will need: digit cards

1. **Ask:** *What is a prime number?* (a number with only two factors) Make sure pupils realise that a prime number has two factors, itself and one. **Ask:** *Can you give an example?*

2. **Ask:** *Do you know what a number that is not prime is called?* (a composite number) **Say:** *A composite number is a number that is not prime.* Say this two or three times so that pupils begin to become familiar with the idea of a composite number.

3. Give each pupil a set of digit cards. **Say:** *Sort your digit cards into numbers that are prime numbers and numbers that are composite numbers. Which numbers are prime? What are their factors? What are the factors of the other numbers? Is it possible for even numbers to be prime?* (two is the only even prime number having two factors, which are two and one; all the other even numbers will have a factor of two as well as others)

4. **Ask:** *What do you think a prime factor is?* (a factor that is a prime number) *Why do you think that?* Guide pupils to say that a prime factor is a factor that is a prime number.

5. **Ask:** *Can you write down the factor pairs for 12?* (1 and 12, 2 and 6, 3 and 4) **Ask:** *Which of these factors are prime numbers?* (2 and 3) *Can you prove it?*

6. Ask pupils to find prime factors of other numbers.

Key check: Do pupils understand the key vocabulary of prime number, composite number and prime factor?

Extension: For each factor pair for 12, pupils factorise each number until all are prime, for example, 12: 3 and 4 are factors of 12, 4 is not prime. We can make it prime by using the equivalent 2 x 3. So the prime factors of 12 are 2, 2 and 3. They then explore prime factors for 24 in the same way.

Support: Focus on working with prime numbers to 10.

Prime or not?

Strand: Number – multiplication and division

Learning objective: To establish whether a number up to 100 is prime and recall prime numbers up to 19.

You will need: paper 100 squares, multiplication square

1. **Ask:** *What is a prime number?* Prompt pupils to say that a prime number has only two factors, itself and one. **Ask:** *Can you give an example? Do you know what a number that is not prime is called?* Prompt pupils to say that a composite number is a number that is not prime. **Ask:** *What is a prime factor?* Prompt pupils to say that a prime factor is a factor that is prime.

2. **Ask:** *Which numbers up to 10 are prime? How do you know?* (2, 3, 5, 7 because they have two factors, one and the number itself)

3. **Say:** *Let's spend some time working with a partner to find the prime numbers between 10 and 20.* Take feedback and ask them to prove that the numbers they think are prime actually are.

4. Give each pupil a paper 100 square and a multiplication square. Pupils work out which numbers from 20 to 100 are prime. They circle each one. They discuss their thinking with a partner and check their thinking on a multiplication square to ensure they haven't included any composite numbers. After a few minutes, take feedback. Look at each number from 20 and work out their factors using their knowledge of multiplication facts. **Ask:** *What do you notice about the numbers you have circled?* (They are found either side of the multiples of six except when the number is a multiple of five such as 25 and 35.)

Key check: Do pupils understand the key vocabulary of prime number, composite number and prime factor?

Extension: Pupils write an explanation to show why it is not possible to make multiplication calculations that have products that are prime numbers. They then write some single-digit and two-digit multiplication calculations and add another number to make the answer a prime number, e.g. (2 × 3) + 1 = 7, (9 × 5) + 2 = 47.

Support: Focus on working with prime numbers to 10.

Multiplication

Strand: Number – multiplication and division

Learning objective: To multiply numbers up to 4 digits by a one- or two-digit number using a formal written method, including long multiplication for two-digit numbers.

You will need: coloured counters (red = 1000, yellow = 100, blue = 10, green = 1), whiteboard, whiteboard pen

1. Ask pupils to use the counters to make 124 and to set them out in a line with five more identical lines underneath, as shown. Draw a grid on the board with the headings 100, 10 and 1, and write 6 on the left.

2. **Ask:** *How can you use your array to work out the answer to 124 × 6?* (work out how many ones, tens and hundreds counters there are) *What are six lots of four?* (24) Write 24 under the ones part of the grid. *What are six lots of 20?* (120) Write this under the 10s section of the grid. *What are six lots of 100?* (600) Write this under the 100s in the grid. *What do we need to do to these values to find the product of 124 multiplied by six?* (Add = 744)

3. Show 124 multiplied by six using the formal written method. **Ask:** *We know 4 × 6 = 24, can we keep 24 in the ones position?* (no because 24 has two tens) Ask pupils to exchange 20 ones for two tens. **Say:** *In your written model, write 4 and place 2 under the tens.* **Ask:** *We know 20 × 6 = 120, can we keep 12 tens in the ones position?* (no because 120 has one hundred) Ask pupils to exchange 10 tens for one hundred. **Ask:** *What do we need to remember to do?* (add the exchanged 2 tens to the other 2 tens) Write 4 in the tens position and 1 under the hundreds. **Ask:** *We know 100 × 6 = 600, what do we need to remember to do?* (add the exchanged hundred to the other 6 hundreds) Write 7 in the hundreds position.

4. Repeat for other three-digit numbers multiplied by a single digit.

Key check: Do pupils understand the process of multiplication? Can they use the formal written method?

Extension: Ask pupils to multiply four-digit numbers by a single-digit number. They use counters and record using the written method.

Support: Focus on multiplying two-digit numbers by a single-digit number. They use counters and record using the written method.

Using known facts

Strand: Number – multiplication and division

Learning objective: To multiply and divide numbers mentally drawing upon known facts.

You will need: whiteboards, whiteboard pens

1. **Ask:** *What is six multiplied by seven? How do you know?* (e.g. recall, recited tables facts, know 6 × 6 = 36 and add another 6) *If we know that 6 × 7 = 42, what else do we know? Can we use commutativity and inverse to make three more facts?* (7 × 6 = 42, 42 ÷ 7 = 6, 42 ÷ 6 = 7) *What else do we know?* (e.g. 6 × 70 = 420, 70 × 6 = 420, 420 ÷ 70 = 6, 420 ÷ 6 = 70, 60 × 7 = 420, 7 × 60 = 420, 420 ÷ 60 = 7, 420 ÷ 7 = 60) *Why do we know these facts?* (e.g. If we multiply one of the numbers to make it 10 times greater, then the product needs to be multiplied by 10 so it is also 10 times greater.)

2. **Say:** *Write down as many new facts as you can from 6 × 7 by multiplying the multiplicand and the product by 100.* For each new fact, pupils write the commutative fact and the two divisions.

3. **Ask:** *What is eight multiplied by nine? How do you know? If we know that 8 × 9 = 72, what else do we know?* (commutative facts and division facts for 8 × 9 = 72, 8 × 90 = 720 and 80 × 9 = 720) *Can we make up more facts by doubling the multiplier? What will we need to do to the product?* (double it: 8 × 18 = 144, 18 × 8 = 144, 144 ÷ 18 = 8, 144 ÷ 8 = 18, etc.)

4. Pupils write down as many new facts as they can by doubling the multiplicand and product for 6 × 7 = 42, ensuring they include the commutative and inverse facts.

5. Repeat the above for four multiplied by seven, but this time halving. Demonstrate for 4 × 7 = 28, 4 × 3.5 = 14.

6. Pupils write down as many new facts as they can by halving the multiplicand and product for 6 × 7 = 42.

Key check: Have pupils remembered what commutativity and inverse are and can they use these to generate new facts?

Extension: Ask pupils to multiply by 10, double and halve to generate new facts for 9 × 7 = 63. They should remember to include the commutative and inverse facts.

Support: Generate new facts by focusing on commutativity, inverse and multiplying by 10 only.

Division

Strand: Number – multiplication and division

Learning objective: To divide numbers up to 4 digits by a one-digit number using the formal written method of short division, and interpret remainders appropriately for the context.

You will need: coloured counters (red = 1000, blue = 100, yellow = 10, green = 1)

1. **Ask:** *What is the inverse of multiplication?* (division) *What do you know about multiplication?* (e.g. repeated addition, adding groups of the multiplier, vocabulary: multiplicand, multiplier, product) *So what do you know about division?* (repeated subtraction, subtracting groups of the divisor, vocabulary: dividend, divisor, quotient, division bracket) Prompt pupils to say that the dividend divided by the divisor equals the quotient.

2. Ask pupils to make 135 using the counters. Explain that they will be dividing this by three. **Ask:** *Can you explain what we are doing when we divide 135 by three?* (finding out how many groups of three there are in 135) *Hold up your one hundred counter. Can we make a group of three one hundred counters?* (We only have one so it can't be done.) *What do you think we need to do?* (exchange the one hundred for 10 tens) Pupils make the exchange.

3. Write 135 divided by three as the formal written method with the division bracket around 135. Cross out 1 and place it beside the 3. **Ask:** *Can we make any groups of 3 out of the 13 tens?* Pupils make the groups. Ensure they are taking groups of three away and not sharing. **Ask:** *How many groups of 3 tens are there? How many are left? What do you think we need to do?* (exchange the ten for ones) Pupils make the exchange. Place 4 above the division bracket in the tens. Cross out 3 on your calculation and place 1 beside the 5. **Say:** *Can we make any groups of 3 out of the 15 ones?* Ask pupils to make the groups. **Ask:** *How many groups of 3 ones are there?* Write 5 above the division bracket in the ones position. **Ask:** *What is 135 divided by 3?*

4. Repeat for other three-digit numbers divided by three.

Key check: Can pupils explain the links between multiplication and division?

Extension: Ask pupils to make four-digit numbers to divide by three.

Support: Work directly with pupils as they divide three-digit numbers by three until they understand the process.

Squares and cubes

Strand: Number – multiplication and division

Learning objective: To recognise and use square numbers and cube numbers, and the notation for squared (^{2}) and cubed (^{3}).

You will need: multiplication square, squared paper, interlocking cubes

1. **Ask:** *What is a square number?* (a number multiplied by itself) *Can you explain how you would work out two squared?* (2 × 2 = 4)

2. Give pupils a multiplication square. They identify the squares of each number from 1 to 12 by sliding two fingers horizontally and vertically from, for example, four and find the number where their fingers meet. **Ask:** *Can you explain how you know these are square numbers? How did your multiplication square help you to find them?*

3. Give each pupil a sheet of squared paper. They use this to show a representation of square numbers. First, they draw a one-by-one square. **Ask:** *Can you explain how this shows $1^2 = 1$?* (one side of 1cm × another side of 1cm gives a square with an area of 1cm^2) Repeat for all squares to 7 × 7.

4. **Ask:** *How do you think we would write one squared using a symbol?* (1^2) *How do our square representations help us know that?* (there are two dimensions, horizontal and vertical)

5. **Ask:** *If you know that a square number is a number multiplied by itself, what do you think a cubed number is?* Show pupils a cube. **Ask:** *What shape is this? How many dimensions does it have? What are they?* (A cube is a three-dimensional shape, with a width, length and height.) *Does this help you to figure out what a cubed number is?* (A number multiplied by itself twice.)

6. **Ask:** *What is two cubed?* (2 × 2 × 2 = 8) *Can you prove this using cubes?* Give pupils interlocking cubes. They make a 2 × 2 × 2 cube. **Ask:** *How many cubes did you use? How do you think we would write two cubed using a symbol?* (2^3) *Why?* (Because we are multiplying the number by itself and then by itself again.)

Key check: Can pupils explain square and cube numbers?

Extension: Ask pupils to explore other cube numbers using the cubes. They record their findings in their own way.

Support: Spend longer focusing on square numbers.

Scaling

Strand: Number – multiplication and division

Learning objective: To solve problems involving multiplication and division, including scaling by simple fractions and problems involving simple rates.

You will need: coloured counters

1. Pupils place one counter on the table and then a line of three below the first one. **Ask:** *If the first counter represents 25, what do the three counters represent? How do you know?* (75 because there are three lots of 25.) *If the three counters represent 600, what does the first counter represent? How do you know?* (200 because you divide 600 by 3.)

2. Pupils place a line of four counters below the first one. **Ask:** *If the first counter represents 32, what do the four counters represent? How do you know?* (128 because there are four lots of 32: double 32 and double again.) *If four counters represent 30, what does the first counter represent? How do you know?* (7.5 by finding a quarter of 30 by halving and halving again.)

3. Tell pupils that they have been scaling up and down. **Ask:** *From what you have been doing, can you explain what scaling up and down is?* (making something greater or smaller by multiplying and dividing)

4. **Ask:** *When would you see scaling in real life?* (e.g. plans of houses: scaling down, photographs of people: scaling down, models of buildings: scaling down, enlargements of insects in photographs: scaling up)

5. **Say:** *Raj had a piece of rope 24m in length and Tom had a piece one third of that length. How long was Tom's rope?* Pupils set the problem out using counters and then solve it. (8m)

6. Set similar problems keeping Raj's length of rope the same, but changing the fraction of Tom's length to one half, and one fifth, one sixth, one tenth, etc. Pupils set out the problem using counters and solve it.

Key check: Can pupils explain the links between scaling and multiplication and division, and also to fractions?

Extension: Pupils make scaling down problems involving fractions to give to a partner to solve.

Support: Focus on scaling down by one half and one quarter only.

IMPACT Intervention
English Activities

Degrees of possibility

Strand: Writing – vocabulary, grammar and punctuation

Learning objective: To use adverbs to indicate degrees of possibility.

You will need: whiteboard, whiteboard pen, six sentences containing adverbs of possibility (to include: surely, perhaps, maybe, certainly, definitely, clearly, undoubtedly, possibly, obviously, probably)

1. **Ask:** *Can you explain what an adverb is?* Agree that an adverb modifies a verb and can say how, where, when or how often something happens. Write some examples on the whiteboard and discuss how each adverb is modifying the verb. For example, Megan eats **slowly**. (how) My book is **upstairs**. (where) I walked to school **yesterday**. (when) I **always** practise my tables at the weekend. (how often)

2. **Say:** *Adverbs can also indicate degrees of possibility.* **Ask:** *What do you think this means?* Agree that these are adverbs that show how certain we are about something.

3. Give pupils six sentences containing adverbs that indicate degrees of possibility. **Ask:** *Which is the adverb(s) in each sentence? Highlight them.*

4. **Ask:** *Is each adverb indicating that something is 'certain' or 'uncertain'?*

5. **Say:** *The adverbs maybe and perhaps usually come at the beginning of the clause. For example,* **Maybe** *I will take the bus.* **Perhaps** *it will rain later.*

6. **Say:** *Other adverbs of possibility usually come either after the verb to be (am, is, are, was, were), for example, He is* **certainly** *very naughty; Noah was* **definitely** *the best choice for team captain, or before the main verb, for example, The dog will* **definitely** *bark when the postman comes; Mia will* **clearly** *win today's cross-country race.*

Key checks: Do pupils know that adverbs can modify a verb, saying how, when, where or how often something happens? Do pupils understand that not all adverbs end in ly (e.g. maybe, perhaps)?

Extension: Pupils write their own sentences containing adverbs of certainty and uncertainty. They compare with their partner, then share with the rest of the group.

Support: Provide less able spellers with a word bank of the adverbs that indicate degrees of possibility.

Relative clauses I

Strand: Writing – vocabulary, grammar and punctuation

Learning objective: To know that a relative clause is a type of subordinate clause which begins with a relative pronoun (who, which, where, when, whose, that).

You will need: whiteboard, sentence strips (see step 4), whiteboards and pens

1. **Ask:** *Can you name the relative pronouns?* Write them on the whiteboard as pupils say them. (who, that, which, where, when, whose)

2. Display a sentence, for example: 'The book, which you gave me for Christmas, was amazing!' **Ask:** *Can you identify the relative pronoun in the sentence and the noun to which the relative pronoun refers?* (*which* and *The book*)

3. **Ask:** *What is a relative clause?* **Say:** *A relative clause provides extra information about the subject in a sentence. It is introduced by a relative pronoun and is a type of subordinate clause.* **Ask:** *Which is the relative clause in the displayed sentence?* ('which you gave me for Christmas') **Ask:** *Does it make sense on its own?* (no) **Ask:** *Does 'The book was amazing!' make sense on its own?* (yes) **Ask:** *What do we call this clause?* (the main clause)

4. Give pupils sentences containing relative clauses, which have been cut into three parts and shuffled (examples below). **Ask:** *Can you put the sentence strips back together to make sentences containing relative clauses? Can you add commas in the right places?*

Main clause		Relative clause
The huge tree	fell across the river.	which was struck by lightning
My little sister	cried all night.	who has toothache
The teacher	retired last week.	who had been at the school for 30 years

---

Key checks: Can pupils name and spell the relative pronouns? Do they understand that a relative pronoun refers back to a preceding noun or clause? Do they know that a relative clause provides extra information about the subject of a sentence? Do they know that it is a type of subordinate clause, introduced by a relative pronoun, and does not make sense on its own? Do they know that a main clause makes sense on its own?

Extension: Pupils make up their own sentences containing a relative clause.

Support: Recap what is meant by the terms noun, subject and subordinate clause.

Relative clauses II

Strand: Writing – vocabulary, grammar and punctuation

Learning objective: To understand that a relative pronoun is often implied (omitted).

You will need: whiteboard, whiteboard pens, cards with relative pronouns (one set per pair)

1. **Ask:** *Can you name the relative pronouns?* (who, that, which, where, when, whose)

2. **Ask:** *Can you write the following sentence a different way?* Display: 'The car that my uncle bought is red.' Discuss and then **say:** *The relative pronoun that can be omitted.* Display and discuss more sentences where the relative pronoun can be omitted.

3. Give pairs of pupils a set of relative pronoun cards. **Say:** *Place your cards face down and take turns to choose one* (e.g. when) *and make up and write down a sentence containing it* (e.g. The year when I was born is famous for many other reasons!).

4. **Ask:** *Which relative pronouns in your sentences can be omitted?* (e.g. The year I was born is famous for many other reasons!)

5. **Ask:** *Have you written any sentences where you can't omit the relative pronoun? For example, Mr Smith, whose cat ran away, is thrilled she has returned.* **Ask:** *Would this sentence work if we omitted the pronoun?* Agree that this does not work. Allow pupils time to decide if they have a sentence where the pronoun cannot be omitted. Check some examples.

6. **Say:** *Some sentences will need slight changes to be made if you remove the relative pronoun.* Write 'My little sister, who was wearing flip flops, tripped and cut her toe.' **Ask:** *How would this need to be changed?* (My little sister, wearing flip flops, tripped and cut her toe.) **Say:** *As well as the relative pronoun who, the word was has also been omitted.*

Key checks: Do pupils understand that a relative pronoun is often omitted and sometimes they need to make changes so that the sentence makes sense?

Extension: Ask pupils to insert the missing relative pronoun into sentences where these have been omitted.

Support: Give less able pupils sentences where the omission of the relative pronoun requires no further change, until they are more confident. (e.g. 'My dog found the bone that he buried.' → 'My dog found the bone he buried.')

Cohesion I

Strand: Writing – vocabulary, grammar and punctuation

Learning objective: To understand how to use devices to build cohesion within a paragraph using then, after that, this, firstly.

You will need: whiteboard, whiteboard pen, short paragraphs (see steps 1 and 3), sentence strips (see step 4)

1. Display a short paragraph of a recount. For example:

    Yesterday, our class walked to the woods. Firstly, we gathered some branches and stacked them next to a big tree. Then, we made shelters by tying the branches together using some bendy twigs. This meant we used only natural resources. After that, we sat in our shelters while our teacher took photographs.

    Ask: Which *words build cohesion, or help the paragraph 'stick' together, so that the events are in a chronological order?* (Yesterday, Firstly, Then, This, After that) *Let's underline the words.*

2. Display the same paragraph without the cohesive devices:

    Our class walked to the woods. We gathered some branches and stacked them next to a big tree. We made shelters by tying the branches together using some bendy twigs. We used only natural resources. We sat in our shelters while our teacher took photographs.

    Ask: *Does this paragraph flow as well as the first one?* Discuss the repetitive use of the personal pronoun 'we' as the first word in each new sentence.

3. Give pupils a short paragraph where no cohesive devices have been used. For example:

    At the weekend, we are going camping. _____, Dad will pack the tent and our bags in the boot of the car. _____, Mum will read the map and decide which is the best route. _____ should mean we won't get lost like last year! _____, we will set off as early as possible to avoid the traffic.

    Ask: *Can you insert some of the devices used in the first paragraph to improve the cohesion of the paragraph?*

Continues

4. Give pupils sentences, linked using cohesive devices, that have been cut up from a paragraph and shuffled. For example, a paragraph linked to science or geography. **Ask:** *Can you piece these sentences together to form a paragraph? Use the cohesive words to help you.* For example:

Rivers begin at their source, in higher areas such as mountains or hills.
Firstly, rain falling in highland areas flows downward to form a spring or stream.
This then travels downhill where it joins other streams.
The streams then join larger streams; the smaller stream is called a tributary.
When larger streams are fed by lots of tributaries, they become rivers.
The river grows larger as it collects more and more water from the tributaries.
It continues its long journey downhill.
After that, the river flows into an ocean, sea or lake.

Display the paragraph in the correct order and ask pupils to check against their own.

Key checks: Do pupils know how to use then, after that, this and firstly within a paragraph to build cohesion?

Extension: Ask: *Can you make up your own short paragraph using the cohesive devices we have been looking at?*

Support: Give less able pupils only the sentences containing cohesive devices in step 4.

Cohesion II

Strand: Writing – vocabulary, grammar and punctuation

Learning objective: To understand how to use devices to build cohesion across paragraphs using adverbials of time and frequency.

You will need: whiteboard, small whiteboards, whiteboard pens, paragraphs that can be linked using adverbials of time (see step 4), adverbials of time word bank (later, next, last night, yesterday, next summer, tomorrow, last time, often, usually, frequently, all the time, sometimes, in the morning, this week)

1. **Ask:** *What do adverbials of time tell us about the verb in a sentence?* (when or how often something happens/happened)

2. **Ask:** *What examples of adverbials of time can you think of?* Once pupils have exhausted their own suggestions, display the adverbial word bank.

3. **Ask:** *What does cohesion mean?* (sticking together, literally) **Ask:** *What does it mean when I say you need to write a cohesive text?* Discuss and then **say:** *A text has cohesion if it is clear how its separate parts fit, or 'stick', together in a logical order. Using adverbials is one way of creating cohesion.*

4. Display three or four short paragraphs linked by a fronted adverbial of time. **Ask:** *Can you highlight the adverbials?* For example:

    Last week, we learned about gases in science. We discovered…

    This week, we have been learning about…

    Usually, we write up our investigations in our books.

    Next week, we are going to…

    Ask: *Can you highlight the adverbials? How do they aid cohesion?*

5. Display three more short paragraphs that need fronted adverbials of time to link them. **Ask:** *Can you use some of the adverbials in the word bank to link the paragraphs?* **Ask:** *How do these adverbials help your writing?* (make the order clear and help the writing flow)

Key checks: Do pupils know how to use adverbials of time and frequency to build cohesion across paragraphs?

Extension: Ask: *What is the rule about starting a sentence with an adverbial?* If necessary, get pupils to find examples in their reading books. Agree that a fronted adverbial is followed by a comma.

Support: Provide only the correct fronted adverbials, but in a random order.

Cohesion III

Strand: Writing – vocabulary, grammar and punctuation

Learning objective: To understand how to use devices to build cohesion across paragraphs using adverbials of place and number.

You will need: whiteboard and small whiteboards, whiteboard pens, short paragraphs linked by adverbials of place and number (see step 2), a recipe (see step 4)

1. **Ask:** *What do adverbials of place tell us about the verb in a sentence?* Agree that they tell us **where** something happens/happened. **Ask:** *Can you think of any adverbials of place?* Write these on the whiteboard.

2. Display short paragraphs linked by adverbials of place, for example:

   > Far away, a dragon roamed. It roared and blew flames from its nostrils.
   > Down in the valley, the villagers….
   > On the other side of the mountains, a knight paced in the palace gardens …

   Highlight the adverbials and discuss how they aid cohesion.

3. **Ask:** *What do adverbials of number tell us about the verb in a sentence?* Agree they tell us **the order** in which something happens/happened.

4. Display a recipe for making cheese sandwiches, for example:

   > First, butter two slices of bread.
   > Secondly, grate some cheese onto one of the slices.
   > Thirdly, put the second slice on top of the first slice.
   > Fourthly, cut the sandwich into four.
   > Finally, eat and enjoy!

   Ask: *What are the adverbials of number in the recipe? What do they tell us?*

5. **Ask:** *Can you create three or four short paragraphs of your own starting with adverbials of place to describe your school grounds?* Pupils then swap with their partner who underlines the adverbials.

Key checks: Can pupils identify and use adverbials of place and number to build cohesion across paragraphs?

Extension: Ask: *Can you write the steps for a science investigation or a recipe using adverbials of number?*

Support: Provide a bank of adverbials of place to support independent writing.

Tense consistency I

Strand: Writing – vocabulary, grammar and punctuation

Learning objective: To ensure consistent and correct use of tense throughout a piece of writing.

You will need: whiteboard, whiteboard pen, sentence starters (e.g. The naughty puppy, Erin and Stella) and endings (e.g. Mum's slipper. on the trampoline.) on strips of paper, blank strips of paper

1. **Ask:** *What is a verb? Can you tell me what we mean by the present tense?*

2. Display these sentences: 'The grandfather clock ticks.' 'We eat our breakfast in the kitchen.' **Ask:** *Can you tell me the verb in each sentence? What tense is used? Can you write the sentences a different way but still in the present tense?* Check pupils have written 'The grandfather clock **is ticking**.' 'We **are eating** our breakfast in the kitchen.' **Ask:** *What do we call this tense?* (progressive present tense)

3. **Ask:** *When do we use the progressive present tense?* Discuss and then **say:** *We use it when we are talking about something that is a continuous action in the present.*

4. Give pupils the sentence starters and ending strips, and blank strips. **Ask:** *Can you work with a partner to match up the sentence starters and endings, then join them by writing a suitable verb in the simple present tense on your blank strip?* **Say:** *Now turn your verb strip over and rewrite your verb in the present progressive.* **Ask:** *What is the difference in meaning or time scale between the sentences in the present and the progressive present tense?*

5. Read these sentences. **Ask:** *Can you identify the verbs that are not used correctly in the context of each sentence? What should they be?*
   - My mum is drinking tea in the morning.
   - Usually, we are taking the bus to school.
   - We are brushing our teeth after we have eaten breakfast.

Key checks: Do pupils know what a verb is and what is meant by the (simple) present tense and the progressive present tense?

Extension: Pupils make up some of their own sentences using the progressive present tense.

Support: Provide a verb word bank for the activity (e.g. chew, bounce).

Tense consistency II

Strand: Writing – vocabulary, grammar and punctuation

Learning objective: To ensure consistent and correct use of tense throughout a piece of writing.

You will need: whiteboards, whiteboard pens, cloze sentences (see step 5)

1. **Ask:** *What is a verb? Can you tell me what we mean by the past tense?*
2. Display these sentences: 'Our dog barked at the boy.' 'The thieves ran down the road.' **Ask:** *Can you tell me the verb in each sentence? What tense is being used? Can you write the sentences a different way but still in the past tense?* ('Our dog **was barking** at the boy.' 'The thieves **were running** down the road.') **Ask:** *What do we call this tense?* (progressive past)
3. **Ask:** *When do we use the progressive past tense?* Discuss and then **say:** *We use it when we are talking about something that is a continuous action in the past. We also use it to show a continuous action interrupted by a short action, or a continuous action in the past used with an adverbial of time.*
4. Display a sentence where a continuous action is interrupted by a short action, e.g. 'Sami was listening to music when Mia called round.' **Ask:** *What is the continuous action? What is the short action?*
5. Give pupils cloze sentences to complete with the progressive past tense, for example:
   - When Mum arrived home, we _____ (work) hard on our spelling.
   - As I _____ (watch) TV, the phone rang.
   - The sun _____ (shine) all day.
6. Display a short paragraph where tense is not used correctly or consistently. **Ask:** *Which verb tenses are incorrect? What should they be?* For example:

   > Last week, I was taking the bus to the swimming pool with Polly. We waited at the desk when we were meeting Mike. He was deciding to come with us. (Last week, I took the bus to the swimming pool with Polly. We were waiting at the desk when we met Mike. He decided to come with us.)

Key checks: Do pupils know what a verb is and what is meant by the (simple) past tense and the progressive past tense and how to use them correctly?

Extension: Say: *Look through your reading book and find examples of the (simple) past and progressive past tense.*

Support: Ensure subject-verb agreement (e.g. He was running… as opposed to: He were running…)

Past perfect

Strand: Writing – vocabulary, grammar and punctuation

Learning objective To ensure consistent and correct use of tense throughout a piece of writing.

You will need: whiteboard, whiteboard pen, sentences with missing verbs (for step 6)

1. **Ask:** *Which sentence is correct?* 'Mum knew she had met the lady before.' 'Mum knew she has met the lady before.'

2. **Ask:** *Do you know what these verb forms are called?* Display another sentence pair, this time annotating the past perfect and present perfect verb forms.
   - 'Rory was happy when he had finished his book.' (past perfect)
   - 'Rory was happy when he has finished his book.' (present perfect)

3. **Ask:** *Which sentence is grammatically correct?* Discuss and **say:** *The first is correct because the past perfect shows an action that was completed at a point in the past before something else happened. So, Rory finished his book (first action) and then he felt happy (second action).*

4. **Ask:** *How is the past perfect tense form made?* (with the past tense of the verb have + the past participle of the main verb, e.g. had eaten, had thought)

5. Display sentences containing a choice of verb forms. **Ask:** *Can you tell me which is the past perfect tense in each case?* For example: We could see that the bewildered puppy has lost / had lost / was losing its owner.

6. **Say:** *This sentence is missing its verb. Can you complete the sentence using the past perfect tense?* As I _____ (eat) everything on my plate, Mum said I could play outside. Repeat with other sentences.

Key checks: Do pupils know what a verb is and what is meant by the past perfect tense? Do they know when and why to use the past perfect tense?

Extension: Pupils share their weekend experiences and record the range of past tenses they have used.

Support: Provide less able pupils with the past participle of the verb to support the activity in step 6. (e.g. As I _____ (eaten)...)

Modal verbs

Strand: Writing – vocabulary, grammar and punctuation

Learning objective: To indicate degrees of possibility using modal verbs.

You will need: whiteboard, whiteboard pen, sentences on separate strips of paper containing modal verbs indicating certainty, possibility and uncertainty

1. Display sentences containing modal verbs that show degrees of possibility. For example:
   - We might go swimming tomorrow.
   - Diving off the top board can be fun!
   - Dad will take us after he has finished work.

   Ask: *Which word in each sentence tells you that the event is certain or uncertain? Do you know what we call these words?* (modal verbs) Display a list of modal verbs: can, could, will, would, might, may, must, should, shall.

2. Underline the modal verbs in the displayed sentences in step 1. **Ask:** *What comes after the modal verb in each case?* Discuss and **say:** *A verb in its basic – or infinitive – form follows the modal verb.*

3. Display two further sentences containing modal verbs. **Ask:** *Can you tell me the modal verb and circle the verb that follows?*

4. **Ask:** *Can you group the five sentences under the headings 'Certain' and 'Uncertain'?*

5. On the whiteboard, display sentences with a choice of modal verbs, one indicating certainty and one indicating uncertainty. For example:
   - We will / may go to Scotland on holiday this year.
   - Mia might / shall walk the dog today.

   Ask: *Can you write the modal verb that indicates certainty in each sentence?*

6. **Ask:** *Can you write two sentences of your own, and place them under each heading?*

Key checks: Do pupils understand that modal verbs can indicate degrees of possibility? Do pupils know that a modal verb is followed by a verb in its infinitive form?

Extension: Ask: *Can you think of any adverbs that indicate degrees of possibility?*

Support: Demonstrate to pupils that the modal verb 'can' can mean certain or possible (e.g. The weather can be unsettled at this time of year. Mum says we can stay up late tonight.). We also use 'can't' to show certainty (e.g. It can't be 11 o'clock already.).

Commas

Strand: Writing – vocabulary, grammar and punctuation

Learning objective: To use commas to clarify meaning or avoid ambiguity in writing.

You will need: whiteboard, whiteboard pens, sentence strips (see step 6)

1. Display the sentence: 'Nala the girl who fell off her bike has a bandage on her wrist.' **Ask:** *Where would you put commas to make the meaning clearer? Is it Nala the girl comma who... or is it Nala comma the girl who...?*

2. **Ask:** *What does ambiguity mean?* Invite feedback. **Say:** *If something is ambiguous, it means there is more than one possible meaning. We can avoid ambiguity by using commas correctly in our writing.*

3. Display the sentence 'My favourite hobbies are cooking my pets and football.' **Ask:** *What does the writer really mean? Where should the comma be placed to make this clear?*

4. **Ask:** *Can you identify the correctly punctuated sentence in each pair?* Display for example:
   - "Let's eat Grandma!" shouted the children.
   - "Let's eat, Grandma!" shouted the children.

5. Discuss the difference in meaning in each pair. **Ask:** *Why is it important to use commas to clarify meaning?*

6. Provide pupils with sentence strips where the commas are missing and therefore the meaning of each is unclear or ambiguous. **Ask:** *Can you work with your partner to add any missing commas to the sentences?* For example:
   - Our teacher said, "Today, we are learning to cut and paste children."
   - Roy thought the teacher was getting better at spelling.
   - After they left Uncle David Amira and Jackson built a camp.

Key checks: Do pupils understand the importance of using commas to avoid ambiguity and to clarify meaning?

Extension: Ask: *Where else do we use commas?* (To separate items in a list, in direct speech, to mark the boundary between independent clauses and in parenthesis.)

Support: Help pupils to write commas that are oriented and positioned correctly.

Brackets, dashes and commas

Strand: Writing – vocabulary, grammar and punctuation

Learning objective: To use brackets, dashes or commas to indicate parenthesis.

You will need: whiteboard, whiteboard pen, a range of sentences

1. **Ask:** *Can you tell me what 'parenthesis' means?* Take feedback, then **say:** *Parenthesis is when we insert extra information in a sentence.*

2. Write a sentence containing a relative clause. (e.g. 'My uncle's dog, who is still a puppy, chewed my new shoes.') **Ask:** *Which part of the sentence acts like an afterthought or an explanation?* Discuss, then **say:** *The clause 'who is still a puppy' is parenthesis because the rest of the sentence makes sense without it.*

3. **Ask:** *What punctuation marks indicate parenthesis in the sentence?* (commas) *Could you use any other punctuation marks?* Write the sentence again: 'My uncle's dog (who is still a puppy) chewed my new shoes.' **Ask:** *What do we call the punctuation marks that have replaced the commas?* (brackets)

4. **Ask:** *What else could I use instead of brackets?* Write the sentence again: 'My uncle's dog – who is still a puppy – chewed my new shoes.' **Ask:** *What do we call the punctuation marks that have replaced the brackets?* (dashes)

5. **Ask:** *Do we need the whole of the relative clause or could we omit some words?* Discuss and agree that 'who is' could be omitted: 'My uncle's dog, still a puppy, chewed my new shoes.'

6. Pupils correct sentences where the punctuation to indicate a parenthetic clause or word is incorrect or missing. For example:
   - Our – picnic sandwiches, crisps and ice-cream was absolutely – delicious.
   - My cat Tabatha (likes to sleep) next to the fire.

Key checks: Do pupils understand that when the parenthesis is taken out of the sentence, what remains still makes sense?

Extension: Ask: *Do brackets only come in the middle of a sentence? Can you think of any examples where they don't?* For example, We have booked the same restaurant (even though our last meal wasn't great).

Support: Ask pupils to look for examples of parenthesis in their reading books.

Prefixes dis- and mis-

Strand: Writing – transcription

Learning objective: To use further prefixes and understand the guidance for adding them to change the meaning of verbs: dis- and mis-.

You will need: whiteboard, whiteboard pen, a selection of root words that take the prefixes dis- and mis-, a two-column table per pupil or pair with headings 'dis- (makes an opposite word or antonym)' and 'mis- (wrongly/badly or negative word)'

1. **Ask:** *What is a prefix?* (a group of letters added to the start of a word to change its meaning) *What is a verb?* (a word for an action or state of being)

2. Display the prefixes dis- and mis-. **Ask:** *What words can you think of which start with the prefixes dis- and mis-?* Write pupils' suggestions, grouping words with like prefixes together.

3. **Say:** *Look at the root word. What can you tell me about the meaning of the root word compared with its meaning with the prefix?* Display and explain the words 'opposite', 'antonym' and 'negative' using examples of root words and the new words with the prefixes added.

4. Give pupils a jumbled selection of root words that take the prefixes dis- and mis- (e.g. agree, behave, believe, use, approve, time). **Say:** *Can you (independently or with a partner) add the appropriate prefix to each root word then write it in the correct column in the table provided?*

5. **Ask:** *Can you make up a sentence containing each of your words?* Pupils read out their sentences; the group feeds back.

Key checks: Can pupils use the prefixes dis- and mis- to change the meaning of verbs? Do they understand that the spelling of the root word does not change?

Extension: Pupils make lists of verbs starting with these prefixes that appear in independent reading.

Support: Remind pupils that if the prefix ends with the same letter that the root word begins with, both letters are kept (e.g. misspell).

Prefixes de-, re- and over-

Strand: Writing – transcription

Learning objective: To use further prefixes and understand the guidance for adding them to change the meaning of verbs: de-, re- and over-.

You will need: whiteboard, whiteboard pen, a selection of root words that take the prefixes de-, re- and over-, a three-column table per pupil or pair with the headings 'de- (undo something)', 're- (do something again)' and 'over- (do something too much)'

1. **Ask:** *What is a prefix? What is a verb?*

2. Display the prefixes de-, re- and over-. **Ask:** *What words can you think of which start with the prefixes de-, re- and over-?* Write pupils' suggestions, grouping words with like prefixes together.

3. **Say:** *Look at the root word. What can you tell me about the meaning of the root word compared with its meaning with the prefix?* Display the phrases: 'undo something', 'do something again' and 'do something too much'. Ask: *Which prefix do we use when we want to change the meaning of a root word to mean undo?* (de-) *And to change the meaning to do something again?* (re-) *And to change the meaning to do something too much?* (over-)

4. Give pupils a jumbled selection of root words that take the prefixes de-, re- and over- (e.g. frost, pay, arrange, react, compose, cycle). **Say:** *Can you (independently or with a partner) add the appropriate prefix to each root word then write it in the correct column in the table provided?*

5. **Ask:** *Can you make up a sentence containing each of your words?* Pupils read out their sentences; the group feeds back.

Key checks: Can pupils use the prefixes de-, re- and over- to change the meaning of verbs? Do they understand that the spelling of the root word does not change?

Extension: Pupils make lists of verbs starting with these prefixes that they come across in independent reading.

Support: Remind pupils that if the prefix ends with the same letter that the root word begins with, both letters are kept (e.g. overreact).

Prefixes that come from Latin and Greek

Strand: Writing – transcription

Learning objective: To understand the history of words and the relationships between them to help spelling.

You will need: whiteboard, whiteboard pen, a range of words to display

1. **Ask:** *Can you name any words that start with prefixes that come from Latin or Greek?* Write any appropriate suggestions on a whiteboard, grouping words with like prefixes together. Add to the list (e.g. submarine, telescope, bicycle, autograph).

2. Display subway and submerge and **ask:** *What is a subway? What does submerge mean? What do you think the prefix sub- means?* Agree that sub means below or under and comes from Latin.

3. Display television and telephone and **ask:** *What is a television? What is a telephone? What do you think the prefix tele- means?* Agree that tele means distant and comes from Greek.

4. Display binoculars and bilingual and **ask:** *What are binoculars? What does bilingual mean? What do you think the prefix bi- means?* Agree that bi means two and comes from Latin.

5. Display autobiography and autopilot and **ask:** *What is an autobiography? What does autopilot mean? What do you think auto means?* Agree that auto means self and comes from Greek.

6. Display words containing number prefixes: **tri**plets, **quin**tuplets, **quad**ruplets, **sex**tuplets. **Ask:** *Can you tell me what each prefix means? Can you tell me a mathematical shape that starts with tri? How many sides/angles has it got? Can you tell me a type of bike that starts with quad? How many wheels does it have? If deca comes from the Greek meaning ten, how many sides will a decahedron have?*

Key checks: Can pupils use their knowledge of some Latin and Greek prefixes to help them with the meaning of a range of words?

Extension: Pupils use a dictionary to establish the meaning of the Latin and Greek prefixes hemi- and mono-.

Support: When less able pupils come across these prefixes in reading, **ask:** *What does that prefix mean?*

Suffixes I

Strand: Writing – transcription

Learning objective: To convert nouns into verbs using suffixes.

You will need: whiteboard, whiteboard pen, suffix table (see step 5), dictionaries

1. **Ask:** *What is a suffix?* (a group of words added to the end of a word to change its meaning) *Can you give me any examples of words that have a suffix?* Write given examples and discuss.

2. **Ask:** *What is a noun? What is a verb?* (noun: naming word for people, places, animals and things; verb: a word for an action or state of being)

3. Write **advert** on the whiteboard. **Ask:** *What suffix can we add to the word advert to convert it into a verb?* Add the suffix -ise to the word advert.

4. Display nouns which already have a suffix attached to the root word (e.g. intensity, donation). **Ask:** *How can we convert these nouns into verbs using the given suffixes?* Demonstrate how to remove the suffix and change the ending to create intens**ify** and don**ate**. **Ask:** *Can you make a sentence using each verb?*

5. Provide a table for pupils to complete. Supply dictionaries if necessary. For example:

-ate		-ise		-ify		-en	
noun	verb	noun	verb	noun	verb	noun	verb
origin		criminal		class		fright	
assassin		final		note		strength	
difference		penalty		terror		length	

6. **Ask:** *Which words did you have to make spelling adjustments to before you could add the suffix?*

7. Give each pupil in the group one verb with which to make a sentence.

Key checks: Can pupils convert a range of nouns into verbs using the suffixes -ate, -ise, -ify and -en, and spell them accurately?

Extension: Ask: *What about the nouns substance and verification? Can you use a dictionary to convert them into verbs?*

Support: Provide words where no change to the root word is required.

Suffixes II

Strand: Writing – transcription

Learning objective: To convert adjectives into verbs using suffixes.

You will need: whiteboard, whiteboard pen, table with the column headings -ate, -ise, -ify, -en (see step 6)

1. **Ask:** *What is a suffix? Can you give me any examples of words that have a suffix?* Write given examples and discuss.
2. **Ask:** *What is an adjective?* (a word that describes a noun) *What is a verb?* (a word for an action or state of being)
3. Write **soft** on the whiteboard. **Ask:** *What suffix can we add to the adjective soft to convert it into a verb?* Add the suffix -en to the word soft.
4. Display adjectives which can take the given suffixes (e.g. pure, equal, active, sad). **Ask:** *How can we convert these adjectives into verbs using the given suffixes?* Demonstrate how to create the verbs purify, equalise, activate and sadden using the suffixes. **Ask:** *What do you notice about the verb sadden?* (that the d has been doubled)
5. **Ask:** *Can you work with a partner to make a sentence using each verb?*
6. Present a table for pupils to complete. For example:

-ate		-ise		-ify		-en	
adjective	verb	adjective	verb	adjective	verb	adjective	verb
different		personal		intense		straight	
captive		material		electric		weak	
appreciative		standard		solid		dead	

7. **Ask:** *Which words did you have to make spelling adjustments to before you could add the suffix?*
8. Give each pupil in the group one verb with which to make a sentence. Pupils take turns to read out their completed sentence.

Key checks: Can pupils convert a range of adjectives into verbs using suffixes -ate, -ise, -ify and -en, and spell them accurately?

Extension: Ask: *What about the adjectives apologetic and medical? Can you use a dictionary to convert them into verbs?*

Support: Ask: *What spelling rule can you make for adjectives ending in 'e'?*

Morphology and etymology

Strand: Writing – transcription

Learning objective: To use knowledge of morphology and etymology in spelling.

You will need: whiteboard, whiteboard pen, word cards (see step 5), A3 paper, dictionaries

1. **Ask:** *What does morphology mean?* Discuss and then **say:** *Morphology is a word's internal make-up, how it is formed, for example with a root word and suffixes or prefixes.* **Ask:** *What is a root word?* Agree that words with the same root can be grouped into word families. **Ask:** *Can you give any examples?* Elicit examples and/or display: medicine, medical, medication, medicinal.

2. **Ask:** *What does etymology mean?* Discuss and then **say:** *Etymology means the history of a word; many words in English have come from Greek, Latin or French.*

3. **Ask:** *Why might it be useful to be able to group words with the same root together?* Agree that it can help with the spelling and meaning of new words that have the same root.

4. Display: sign, signature, signal. **Ask:** *What do you notice about the pronunciation of the letter g?* Agree that it is silent in 'sign' but pronounced in the others. **Ask:** *What do you think the root word 'sign' means?* Elicit ideas, then explain that it comes from the Latin meaning marks or indications.

5. Provide pupils with word cards, for example:

disruption	bankrupt	interrupt	erupt
autograph	autobiography	autopilot	autocratic
transport	translate	transform	transatlantic

   Shuffle the cards then **ask:** *Can you group the word cards so that they are in word families?*

6. Give pupils some words on a sheet of A3 (e.g. company, memory, circus). Provide dictionaries if necessary. **Ask:** *How many words can you write around each word that belong in the same word family?* (e.g. accompany, companion, accompaniment; memorable, remember, memorial; circus, circumference, circular)

Continues

7. **Ask:** *How many words can you make that belong to the same word family using the prefix super?* (e.g. superman, superwoman, supermarket, supersonic, superhero) *What do you think super means?*

8. **Say:** *Look at these words with the prefix aqua: aquamarine, aquaplane, aquarium.* **Ask:** *What do you think the prefix aqua means?*

Key checks: *Can pupils group words with the same prefix or root into word families?*

Extension: Say: *Let's look at the root 'fin' in the words 'finish', 'final' and 'infinite'.* **Ask:** *What do you think the Latin root 'fin' means?* Help pupils see that 'fin' means 'end' and explain that the word 'fin' means 'end' in French. **Ask:** *How many words can you name that share the root graph?* (e.g. biography, autobiography, autograph, telegraph, graphic, grapheme) *What do you think graph means?* Help pupils see that graph means 'write'.

Support: Encourage pupils to make connections between more common words (e.g. familiar, family, familiarise and phobia, claustrophobia, agoraphobia).

Silent letters

Strand: Writing – transcription

Learning objective: To spell some words with silent letters.

You will need: whiteboard, small whiteboards, whiteboard pens, words, sentences and a short paragraph (see steps 5–6)

1. **Ask:** *What is a silent letter?* (a letter that appears in a word but is not pronounced)
2. **Ask:** *How many words can you think of that contain a silent letter?* Elicit examples and group on a whiteboard according to each silent letter.
3. **Ask:** *What patterns do you notice?* (e.g. silent s before l; silent n usually follows m; silent t after s; silent c after s)
4. Display words where the silent letter is omitted but indicated (e.g. r_ombus, cas_le, tom_, we_ge, using words that were not suggested in step 2). **Ask:** *What letter would you insert in each word?*
5. Display sentences which contain words with silent letters, and with the silent letters in those words omitted. **Ask:** *Can you spot the words that are spelt incorrectly? Can you write them correctly on your whiteboard?* For example:
   - I cut the cake in haf so we had to pieces.
   - Morag climed to the top of the iland's highest peak.
6. Provide a short paragraph containing words with silent letters. **Ask:** *Can you highlight the silent letters that you find?* Pupils work independently or with a partner. For example:

   > The princess clim<u>b</u>ed up the cliff, her <u>sw</u>ord fas<u>t</u>ened to her belt. She <u>k</u>new a <u>g</u>narled and ugly <u>g</u>nome was <u>g</u>uarding the <u>k</u>night. Moonlight glis<u>t</u>ened on the water below. She crept up behind the <u>g</u>nome and <u>w</u>res<u>t</u>led him to the ground. The <u>k</u>night recognised her and si<u>g</u>hed in relief.

Key checks: Do pupils know what a silent letter is and can they identify words that contain them? Can they spell words with silent letters correctly?

Extension: Ask: *Can you think of any words that start with a silent p?* (e.g. pneumonia, psychic)

Support: Encourage less able pupils to learn the spelling of words with silent letters by saying each sound out loud (e.g. pronouncing the k when saying knot).

Homophones

Strand: Writing – transcription

Learning objective: To continue to distinguish between homophones.

You will need: whiteboard, whiteboard pen, sentences containing homophones (see step 3), table with homophones (see step 4), table with homophones and definition column (see step 5), dictionaries

1. **Ask:** *Can you explain what a homophone is?* Discuss and then **say:** *A homophone is a word that sounds the same as another word but has a different spelling and meaning.*

2. **Ask:** *How many examples of homophones do you know?* Elicit examples and display them on the whiteboard.

3. **Say:** *These sentences contain a choice from a pair of homophones.* **Ask:** *Can you circle the correct homophone in each sentence?*
   - We are expecting better whether/weather tomorrow.
   - Our teacher said we were allowed/aloud to play outside.

4. **Say:** *This table contains homophones without their matching word.* **Ask:** *Can you complete the table by writing a matching homophone for each word?* For example:

Word	Homophone	Word	Homophone
towed		sighed	
seen		heard	
ball		root	

5. **Say:** *This table contains more challenging homophones.* **Ask:** *Can you use a dictionary to complete it?* For example:

Homophones	Definition
vein	
vane	
vain	
coarse	
course	
aisle	
isle	

Continues

6. **Ask:** *With a partner, can you think up a clue for some pairs of homophones?* Give examples, such as:

   rowed – I did this when I was in a boat

   road – we drive to school on this

   Key checks: Can pupils distinguish between most pairs of homophones?

   Extension: Ask: *Can you think of a way to help you distinguish between the homophones principal and principle and stationery and stationary?* (e.g. The principal is my pal; station**e**ry = **e**nvelopes, station**a**ry = **a**t the station)

   Support: Provide less able pupils with strategies to help them distinguish between homophones.

Near homophones and tricky homophones

Strand: Writing – transcription

Learning objective: To distinguish between near-homophones and other words which are often confused.

You will need: whiteboard, whiteboard pens, sentences with near-homophones (step 3), table with near-homophones and definitions column (see step 4), table with tricky homophones, word class and definitions columns (see step 5)

1. **Ask:** *Can you explain what a near-homophone is?* Discuss and then **say:** *A near-homophone is a word that sounds almost the same as another word but has a different spelling and meaning. These words are often confused.*

2. **Ask:** *How many examples of near-homophones do you know?* Display examples on the whiteboard (e.g. quiet, quite; loose, lose; affect, effect). Demonstrate the difference in pronunciation.

3. **Say:** *These sentences contain a choice from a pair of near-homophones.* **Ask:** *Can you circle the correct word in each sentence?*
   - Tina was quiet/quite tired after the cross-country race.
   - Dad asked Mum for advice/advise about the soup he was cooking.

4. **Say:** *This table contains near-homophones.* **Ask:** *Can you use a dictionary to complete the definitions?*

Near-homophone	Definition
device	
devise	
desert	
dessert	

5. **Say:** *Look at the words in this table. These are tricky homophones because their spelling is almost identical, they sound the same but their meaning is different.* **Ask:** *Can you use a dictionary to find out the word class and a definition of each word?*

Homophone	Word class	Definition
practice		
practise		
licence		
license		

Continues

6. **Ask:** *What rule would you follow for spelling the words in the table?* Discuss and then **say:** *Words that end with **ce** are usually nouns, whereas words ending in **se** are usually verbs.*

Key checks: Can pupils distinguish between most pairs of near-homophones and tricky homophones?

Extension: Ask: *Can you create your own 'memory-jogger' for spelling the near-homophones and tricky homophones that you find most challenging?*

Support: Give pupils near-homophone spellings to learn for homework.

Exception words

Strand: Writing – transcription

Learning objective: To understand that the spelling of some words need to be learnt specifically.

You will need: whiteboard, whiteboard pen, table (see step 3), table with *ough* letter string words (see step 5), dictionaries

1. Display a range of words that are tricky to spell (e.g. separate, definite, marvellous). **Ask:** *Why are these words tricky to spell?* Discuss and then **say:** *They have syllables or sounds that are not pronounced – we tend to say seprate, defnit and marvlous.*

2. **Ask:** *What strategies would help you spell these words?* Discuss breaking the word up into syllables and pronouncing each syllable separately.

3. **Say:** *This table contains words where a letter has been omitted.* **Ask:** *Can you work out what letters are missing? Can you write the correct word?*

parlament	
dictionry	
enviroment	
desprate	

4. Remove the table. Call out each word for pupils to write and spell correctly.

5. **Say:** *The next table contains ough words.* **Ask:** *Can you say each word out loud? What has each word got in common?* Discuss and **say:** *All the words contain the letter string ough.* **Ask:** *What is different about the words?* Discuss and **say:** *The letter string ough is pronounced differently in each one.*

ought	rough	trough	though	borough	bough

Continues

6. **Ask:** *Can you think of any other words with the letter string ough that are pronounced the same as each one?* Elicit:

ought	rough	trough	though	borough	bough
bought	tough	cough	although	thorough	plough
thought	enough		dough		
brought					
fought					
nought					

Ask: *What is a trough? What is a borough? What is a bough?* to ensure pupils understand these less common words.

7. Remove displayed words. Call out each word, then say it in the context of a sentence. Pupils write the word. Display the table again. **Ask:** *Have you spelled each word correctly?*

8. Display a range of other tricky words. **Ask:** *What strategies can you think of to help you spell these words?* (e.g. mischievous, conscience, temperature)

Key checks: Do pupils know how to use a range of strategies to help them spell tricky words?

Extension: Provide tricky words spelled phonetically and ask them to spell these correctly (e.g. veeickle – vehicle). Provide dictionaries.

Support: Monitor incorrectly spelled words and add to homework spellings.

Dictionary work

Strand: Writing – transcription

Learning objective: To use dictionaries to check the spelling and meaning of words.

You will need: flipchart/whiteboard, whiteboard pen, dictionaries, sticky notes, table with words spelt incorrectly (see step 6)

1. **Ask:** *Why do we use a dictionary?* (To check the spelling and meaning of a word.) **Ask:** *Would I look at the beginning, middle or end of the dictionary in order to find the meaning of 'treacherous'? What about 'grain'?*

2. **Ask:** *Can you find the word _____ in the dictionary? What other information is provided apart from the meaning?* (word class (e.g. n. = noun), plural, compound words, etc.) Note: Some dictionaries offer antonyms and synonyms too.

3. Provide words that enable pupils to investigate root words and their derivatives (e.g. star, home, earth). **Ask:** *How many derivatives can you find for each word?*

4. In pairs, pupils use their dictionaries to find a given word. Provide sticky notes. **Ask:** *Who can find each word the quickest?* The winning pair is the first to hold up their dictionary with a sticky note indicating the word.

5. Give pupils a range of words that belong to the word classes verbs, adjectives, nouns or adverbs. **Ask:** *Which word class does each word belong to?*

6. Display a selection of words that have been spelled slightly incorrectly and **ask:** *Can you find the correct spelling of the words and their meanings in your dictionaries?* For example:

Incorrect spelling	Correct spelling	Definition
disapear		
acommodation		

Key checks: Are pupils confident using a dictionary to find the spelling and meaning of words?

Extension: Extend the activity in step 6 to include word class and/or antonyms, if dictionaries allow.

Support: Display the alphabet clearly for less able pupils, to support their dictionary work.

More dictionary work

Strand: Writing – transcription

Learning objective: To use the first three or four letters of a word to check spelling, meaning or both of these in a dictionary.

You will need: whiteboards, whiteboard pens, dictionaries, small whiteboards, words displayed in tables (see steps 1–4)

1. **Ask:** *Can you use your dictionary to order these words alphabetically? Write them on your whiteboard.*

grumpy	xylophone
friendly	zebra
hurricane	yacht

   Ask: *What skill do you need to have to do this activity?* Agree that you need to know the alphabet.

2. **Ask:** *Can you use your dictionary to order these words alphabetically? Write them on your whiteboard.*

armadillo	giggle
antagonise	goggle
alphabet	gaggle

3. **Ask:** *Can you use your dictionary to order these words alphabetically? Write them on your whiteboard.*

brand	clean
break	claim
brief	climb

4. **Ask:** *Can you use your dictionary to order these words alphabetically? Write them on your whiteboard.*

pretence	trespass
present	treasure
prepare	trend

Continues

5. **Ask**: *What letter do we need to look at in each case* (i.e. steps 1–4) *to order the words alphabetically?*

6. Display definitions for words that are likely to be tricky for pupils to spell (e.g. a measure of hot or cold (temperature); a healthy plant eaten by vegetarians (vegetable)). **Ask:** *Can you think of the answer then use your dictionary to find the word and spell it correctly on your whiteboard?*

Key checks: Do pupils know how to use the first three or four letters of a word to check its spelling, meaning or both in a dictionary?

Extension: Ask: *Which word would you **not** find in a dictionary between explore and extinguish – extension, explosion or external?*

Support: Display the alphabet clearly for less able pupils, to support their dictionary work.

Thesaurus work

Strand: Writing – transcription

Learning objective: To use a thesaurus.

You will need: whiteboard, thesauruses, small whiteboards, tables with adjectives (see step 4), tables with adverbs (see step 5)

1. **Ask:** *What is a thesaurus? Why might we want to use one?* Discuss and then **say:** *A thesaurus provides a word that has the same or similar meaning to the word being investigated; it can also provide a word that is opposite in meaning to the word being investigated. This supports vocabulary expansion and makes your writing more interesting.*

2. Display: synonym and antonym. **Ask:** *How many synonyms for 'said' can you write on your whiteboard in one minute? Can you use your thesaurus to find any more?* Repeat for other words (e.g. ran).

3. Display words (e.g. strong, eager) and **Ask:** *Can you find antonyms for strong and eager?*

4. Provide a table containing a list of adjectives. **Ask:** *How many synonyms and antonyms can you find for each adjective?* For example:

Adjective	Synonyms	Antonyms
angry		
strange		
old		

5. Provide a table containing a list of adverbs. **Ask:** *How many synonyms and antonyms can you find for each adverb?* For example:

Adverb	Synonyms	Antonyms
bravely		
deliberately		
carefully		

Continues

6. Display some sentences where the words in bold need replacing with more interesting words. **Ask:** *Can you use your thesaurus to find alternative words?* For example:
   - Shila was feeling **tired**.
   - "I'm full of a bad cold," **said** Mum.
   - The winner **walked** onto the stage.
   - I had a **nice** piece of cake.

Key checks: Are pupils confident using a thesaurus to find alternative words or words with opposite meanings? Can they use the terms synonyms and antonyms to describe these words?

Extension: Provide pupils with negative prefixes to add to root words to make antonyms (e.g. legal, appoint, understand).

Support: Ensure that pupils understand that not all synonyms can be used as direct replacements for words – they should be aware of the context.

Information texts

Strand: Reading – comprehension

Learning objective: To read and discuss a range of non-fiction.

You will need: whiteboard, information leaflets and texts, information books, Internet access, factual websites

1. Display and read an information text (e.g. a book about animals in the wild). **Ask:** *What genre is this writing? Is it made-up or factual? What is it trying to do?* Discuss and **say:** *It is non-fiction, specifically, an information text; it is giving us information and facts.*

2. **Ask:** *What are the features of the text?* Elicit examples and create a bulleted list on the whiteboard, for example:
   - title
   - subheadings
   - factual information
   - pictures, diagrams, graphs, maps
   - bullet points

3. Provide some information books. **Ask:** *What other features do information books include?* (e.g. contents page, index, glossary). **Ask:** *What is an index? What is a glossary?*

4. Give each pupil a short information text. Allow them time to read it then **ask:** *Can you explain to your partner what facts you have learned from your text?*

5. **Ask:** *What is a quick way of finding out facts about something?* Agree that you can use the computer/search engine/websites. Display some websites that give information about something (e.g. a particular animal). Choose one and discuss features (e.g. links to other web pages, fact files).

6. Using the chosen website, **ask:** *Can you tell me...? How do you know that...? Why do you think that...? Find two words that mean... Identify the phrase that tells you...* Model answers to questions that pupils find challenging. **Ask:** *Can you make up a question of your own to ask?*

Key checks: Do pupils know where to look in an information book to find something? Can they answer a range of questions on what they have read?

Extension: More able pupils can summarise the main ideas from the text.

Support: Build confidence in less able pupils through questions that focus on direct recall from the text.

Persuasive letters

Strand: Reading – comprehension

Learning objective: To read and discuss a range of non-fiction.

You will need: whiteboard, whiteboard pen, an example of a persuasive letter set out in a formal letter style

1. Display a persuasive letter on the whiteboard. **Ask:** *Whose is the address on the top right hand side? Whose is the address on the left hand side? How is the letter structured?* (date, Dear…, Yours sincerely/Yours faithfully). *When do we use Yours sincerely? When do we use Yours faithfully?*

2. Read the text together. **Ask:** *What is the first paragraph telling you? What is the writer trying to persuade the recipient to do?*

3. **Ask:** *What techniques does the writer use to try to persuade the recipient?* Support pupils by highlighting the various features and asking them to describe or explain. Compile a bulleted list:
   - rhetorical questions
   - emotive language
   - repetition
   - flattery
   - exaggeration

4. **Ask** a range of questions about the text: *Can you tell me…? How do you know that…? Why do you think that…? Find two words that mean… Identify the phrase that tells you…* Model answers to questions that pupils find challenging.

5. **Ask:** *Do you think the writer was persuasive? How could he/she have been more persuasive?*

6. **Ask:** *How would you persuade a grown-up to let you stay up late to watch a film?* Using the displayed features, pupils make a persuasive speech to each other.

Key checks: Do pupils know how to set out a formal letter? Do they know the features of a persuasive letter? Can they answer a range of questions on what they have read?

Extension: More able pupils can summarise the main ideas from the text.

Support: Build confidence in less able pupils through questions that focus on direct recall from the text.

Adverts

Strand: Reading – comprehension

Learning objective: To read and discuss a range of non-fiction.

You will need: whiteboard, whiteboard pen, a selection of different adverts, a leaflet advertising a holiday destination

1. **Ask:** *What is the purpose of an advert? Can you discuss with your partner then report back to the rest of the group?*

2. **Say:** *Look at the adverts. Discuss what you see and read about the product with your partner.* **Ask:** *Can you come up with a list of features?* Elicit answers and display, for example:
   - bold, eye-catching images
   - colourful, bold fonts
   - rhetorical questions
   - alliteration
   - repetition
   - celebrity endorsement
   - special offer or deal

3. Display another advert. **Ask:** *What are the two main things that grab your attention in the advert? What would make you want to buy this product? Which persuasive techniques are used in the advert?*

4. Provide pupils with a leaflet advertising a holiday destination. Read the text together. **Ask:** *Can you highlight the persuasive features used?*

5. Now ask questions about the text. **Ask:** *Can you tell me…? How do you know that…? Why do you think that…? Find two words that mean… Identify the phrase that tells you…*

6. **Ask:** *What eye-catching images and phrases would you include in an advert about your school?* Elicit ideas and discuss as a group.

Key checks: Can pupils name the features of an advert? Do they understand that the aim of an advert is to persuade?

Extension: Ask: *Can you think of an advert you see on the TV? Why is it memorable?*

Support: Build confidence in less able pupils through questions that focus on direct recall from the text.

Newspaper reports

Strand: Reading – comprehension

Learning objective: To read and discuss a range of non-fiction.

You will need: whiteboard, whiteboard pen, a child-friendly newspaper report (e.g. from *First News*)

1. **Ask:** *What is the purpose of a newspaper? Can you discuss with your partner then report back to the rest of the group?* Take feedback and then **say:** *Newspapers provide news stories, some every day, others once a week. They are written in the past tense because they are reporting on something that has already happened.* **Ask:** *What newspaper, if any, do you have at home?*

2. **Say:** *Read the newspaper report. Discuss what is being reported with your partner. Report back to the rest of the group.*

3. **Ask:** *Can you come up with a list of features?* Elicit answers and display, for example:
   - headline
   - by-line
   - lead paragraph – who? where? what? when? why?
   - main body – how?
   - quotes from sources
   - quotes from eye witnesses
   - picture/s and caption/s

4. **Ask:** *What do you notice about the headline?* (short and eye-catching; maybe alliterative) *What about the quotes – what can you tell me about the punctuation? Are all the quotes direct speech or are some indirect? What person and tense is used?*

5. Now ask questions about the text. **Ask:** *Can you tell me…? How do you know that…? Why do you think that…? Find two words that mean… Identify the phrase that tells you…*

6. **Ask:** *Can you distinguish between statements of fact and opinion?* Give examples of both and discuss the difference.

Key checks: Can pupils name the features of a newspaper report? Do they know that the purpose of a newspaper report is to inform the reader of factual events that have happened?

Extension: Ask: *Can you tell me what propaganda is?* Provide dictionaries for support.

Support: Encourage pupils to read and discuss newspapers for children such as *First News*.

Recounts

Strand: Reading – comprehension

Learning objective: To read and discuss a range of non-fiction.

You will need: whiteboard, whiteboard pen, a recount

1. **Ask:** *What is a recount?* Discuss and then **say:** *A recount tells us about something that has happened; it is in chronological order; it may be an account of a visit, an event in history or an autobiography or biography.*

2. **Ask:** *Can you tell your partner in chronological order what you have done from getting up this morning to arriving at school?*

3. **Ask:** *What tense did you use in your recount? What person did you use? What adverbials of time did you use?* Elicit examples and write these on the whiteboard.

4. Display and read a recount. **Ask:** *Can you summarise each paragraph? Which words are challenging? Can you tell from the context what these words might mean? Can you add anything to our list of features?*
   - past tense
   - first or third person
   - adverbials of time
   - opening paragraph
   - summary paragraph

5. **Ask:** *Can you highlight the adverbials of time in the recount? How does the writer make it more interesting rather than just a list of events in order of occurrence?*

6. **Ask** questions about the text: *Can you tell me…? How do you know that…? Why do you think that…? Find two words that mean… Identify the phrase that tells you…*

Key checks: Can pupils name the features of a recount?

Extension: Ask: *Would a report about wild animals be chronological or non-chronological?*

Support: Build confidence in less able pupils through questions that focus on direct recall from the text.

Writing an information text

Strand: Writing – composition

Learning objective: To plan, write, evaluate and edit.

You will need: whiteboard, whiteboard pen, information text, word bank containing subject-specific vocabulary

1. Provide information related to the subject you want the pupils to write about. Read and discuss, and create a word bank. **Ask:** *Can you remember the features of an information text?* Display:
   - title
   - subheadings
   - factual information
   - pictures, diagrams, graphs, maps
   - bold text
   - bullet points

2. **Say:** *You are going to plan, write, evaluate and edit an information text using the following success criteria:*

features of an information text	
variety of sentence starters, lengths and types	
engaging and appropriate content	
a range of accurate punctuation	
interesting language and vocabulary choices	

   Display the success criteria or provide as a grid with tick boxes for each pupil.

3. Model how you would go about planning the text, either as a mind map or a spider diagram. **Say:** *Subheadings can help with paragraphing. So, if my topic is the Sahara Desert, what might my subheadings be?* For example:

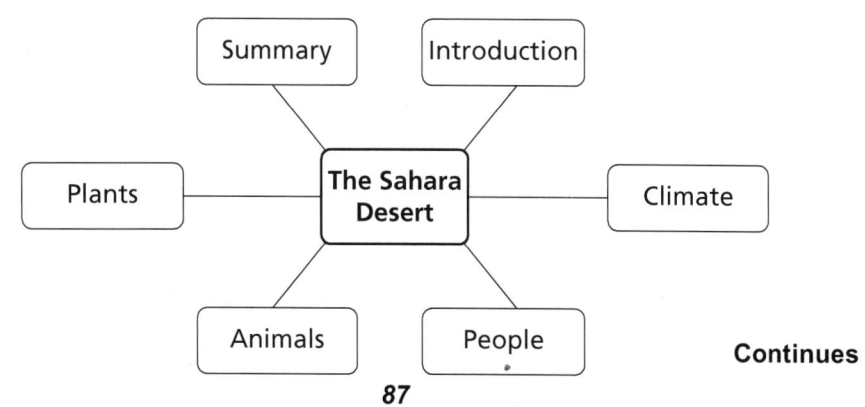

   The Sahara Desert: Summary, Introduction, Climate, People, Animals, Plants

Continues

4. Model an opening paragraph. Start the next paragraph as 'shared writing' – by eliciting suggestions from the pupils. Leave both displayed.

5. Pupils write independently from this point with a partner. Listen to each text. Using peer assessment and the success criteria, evaluate the writing.

6. Pupils self-edit to correct and improve their writing.

Key checks: Can pupils use the appropriate features for this genre?

Extension: Provide a bank of more challenging vocabulary to include in their writing.

Support: Provide some sentence openers.

Writing persuasive letters

Strand: Writing – composition

Learning objective: To plan, write, evaluate and edit.

You will need: whiteboard, whiteboard pen, persuasive letter, word bank containing subject-specific vocabulary

1. Recap the layout of a formal letter and display. Display and read an example of a persuasive letter using the same formal format. **Ask:** *Can you remember the features of persuasive writing?* Display:
   - rhetorical questions
   - emotive language
   - repetition
   - flattery
   - exaggeration

   Highlight examples of the features in the example letter.

2. **Say:** *You are going to plan, write, evaluate and edit a persuasive letter using the following success criteria*:

appropriate features of persuasive writing	
variety of sentence starters, lengths and types	
engaging and appropriate content	
a range of accurate punctuation	
interesting language and vocabulary choices	

   Display the success criteria or provide as a grid with tick boxes for each pupil.

3. Provide a subject you want the pupils to write about and discuss. For example, a letter to the council to complain about plans to build a road through a woodland area.

Continues

4. **Ask:** *What three reasons would you give to persuade the council not to build the road?* Gather ideas and model how you would go about planning the text, either as a mind map or a spider diagram.

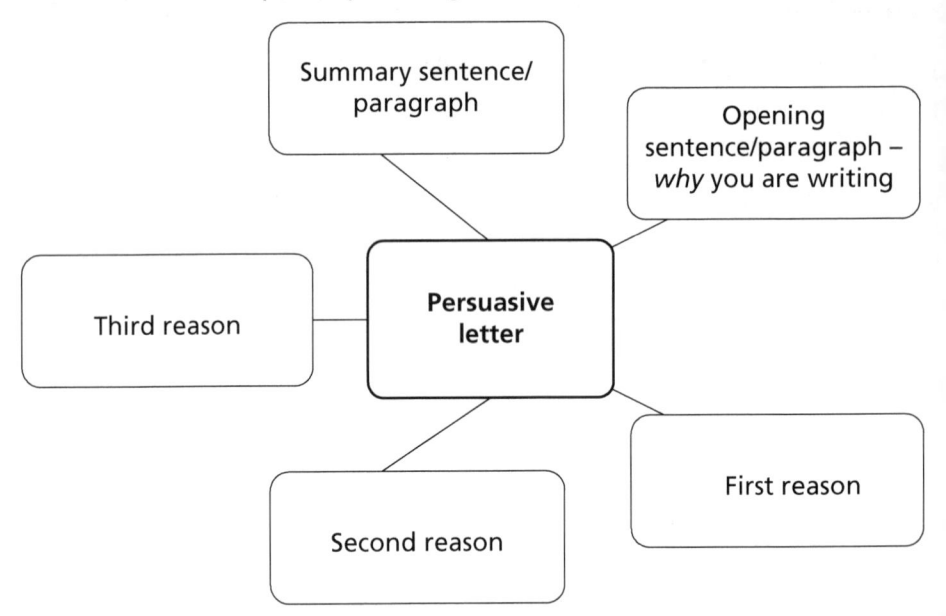

```
                    ┌──────────────────┐
                    │ Summary sentence/│
                    │    paragraph     │        ┌──────────────────┐
                    └──────────────────┘        │     Opening      │
                              │                 │ sentence/paragraph – │
                              │                 │  why you are writing │
                              │                 └──────────────────┘
   ┌──────────────┐      ┌──────────────┐              │
   │ Third reason │──────│  Persuasive  │──────────────┘
   │              │      │    letter    │
   └──────────────┘      └──────────────┘
                              │               ┌──────────────┐
                              │               │ First reason │
                              │               └──────────────┘
                    ┌──────────────────┐
                    │  Second reason   │
                    └──────────────────┘
```

5. Model an opening sentence/paragraph. Start the next paragraph as 'shared writing' – by eliciting suggestions from the pupils. Leave both displayed.

6. Pupils write from this point independently or with a partner. Listen to each text. Using peer assessment and the success criteria, evaluate the writing.

7. Pupils self-edit to correct and improve their writing.

Key checks: Can pupils use the appropriate features for this genre?

Extension: Ask: *How could you have made your writing even better?*

Support: Provide a word bank.

Writing adverts

Strand: Writing – composition

Learning objective: To plan, write, evaluate and edit.

You will need: whiteboard, whiteboard pen, a range of adverts, A3 plain paper, word bank containing subject-specific vocabulary, coloured pen/pencils

1. Provide pupils with examples of adverts related to the subject you have chosen. **Say:** *Look at the adverts. Discuss what you see and read about the product with your partner.*

2. **Ask:** *Can you remember the features of an advert?* Elicit answers and display:
   - bold, eye-catching images
   - colourful, bold fonts
   - rhetorical questions
   - alliteration
   - repetition
   - celebrity endorsement
   - special offer or deal

   Highlight examples in the adverts you are reading.

3. **Say:** *You are going to plan, write, evaluate and edit an advert using the features of this genre.*

4. Provide a subject for the pupils to write their advert about. For example, an advert for a 'healthy' burger. Elicit ideas and discuss as a group.

5. Model how you would plan the advert. For example:
   - product name
   - what makes it healthy?
   - special offer
   - celebrity backing

   Ask: *Where would you put the image? How would you present the product name?* Discuss layout.

6. Pupils create their own adverts independently. They swap with a partner for peer assessment. **Ask:** *Has the advert got most of the features for the genre? What would make you want to buy the product?*

Key checks: Do pupils know the features of an advert?

Extension: Pupils can create an advert for radio which includes a jingle.

Support: Provide a word bank with subject-specific vocabulary.

Writing newspaper reports

Strand: Writing – composition

Learning objective: To plan, write, evaluate and edit.

You will need: whiteboard, whiteboard pen, newspaper reports, A4 or A3 plain paper, word bank containing subject-specific vocabulary, coloured pen/pencils

1. Provide pupils with examples of articles. **Ask:** *Can you remember the features of a newspaper report?* Elicit answers and display:
   - headline
   - by-line
   - lead paragraph (who? where? what? when? why?)
   - main body – how?
   - quotes from sources
   - quotes from eye witnesses
   - picture and caption

2. **Say:** *You are going to plan, write, evaluate and edit a newspaper article using the features of this genre and the following success criteria:*

appropriate features of newspaper reports	
variety of sentence starters, lengths and types	
a range of accurate punctuation	
interesting language and vocabulary choices	
engaging and appropriate content	

Provide a prompt, for example: A computer has been stolen from the school office. The caretaker spotted the thief running away with it and called the police. You are the first reporter on the scene.

3. Planning – Model how to plan a newspaper report and what type of questions pupils should consider asking to obtain their content. For example, using the prompt above, model the questions that could be used to generate planning notes. For example:
What happened? (a computer was stolen from the office at XXXX Primary School)
When did it happen? (Sunday evening)
Who witnessed it? (a lady walking her dog)

Continues

What did the witness say? ("I was walking my dog past the school when I saw a suspicious man running away from the school carrying a computer.")
What was the man wearing? (a blue hoody and jeans)
Why was he able to steal it so easily? (the lock on the door was loose)
Any other sources? (the school caretaker, who said she had been meaning to fix the lock; the head teacher, who said the school would now be checking all locks and installing security cameras)

4. **Say:** *Using our planning notes, can you write your newspaper report about the robbery?* (Provide A4 or A3 paper, folded to form two 'columns'.)

5. Pupils write independently or with a partner. Invite pupils to read their texts aloud and ask others to offer feedback. Using peer assessment and the success criteria, pupils evaluate their writing.

6. Pupils use the feedback to self-edit their writing to correct and improve it. They should check for correct spelling, punctuation and grammar, and make sure their report flows and makes sense.

Key checks: Do pupils know the features of a newspaper report?

Extension: Show headlines that use alliteration. **Ask:** *Can you use alliteration in your headline?* Model: Loose Lock Lets Lout In.

Support: Provide a template for a newspaper article; include paragraph openings and sentence starters.

Writing recounts

Strand: Writing – composition

Learning objective: To plan, write, evaluate and edit.

You will need: whiteboard, whiteboard pen, recounts, word bank containing subject-specific vocabulary

1. Recap – **Ask:** *What is a recount?* Agree that a recount tells us about something that has happened; it is in chronological order; it may be an account of a visit, an event in history or an autobiography or biography.

2. Provide and read a recount. **Ask:** *Can you remember the features of a recount?* Display:
   - past tense
   - first or third person
   - adverbials of time
   - opening paragraph
   - summary paragraph

   Highlight examples in the text you have read.

3. **Say:** *You are going to plan, write, evaluate and edit a recount using the features of this genre and the following success criteria:*

appropriate features of a recount	
variety of sentence starters, lengths and types	
engaging and appropriate content	
a range of accurate punctuation	
interesting language and vocabulary choices	

Provide a prompt (e.g. a school trip or a biography of someone pupils have already researched and gathered facts about).

Continues

4. Model how to plan the text, either with a mind map or a spider diagram.

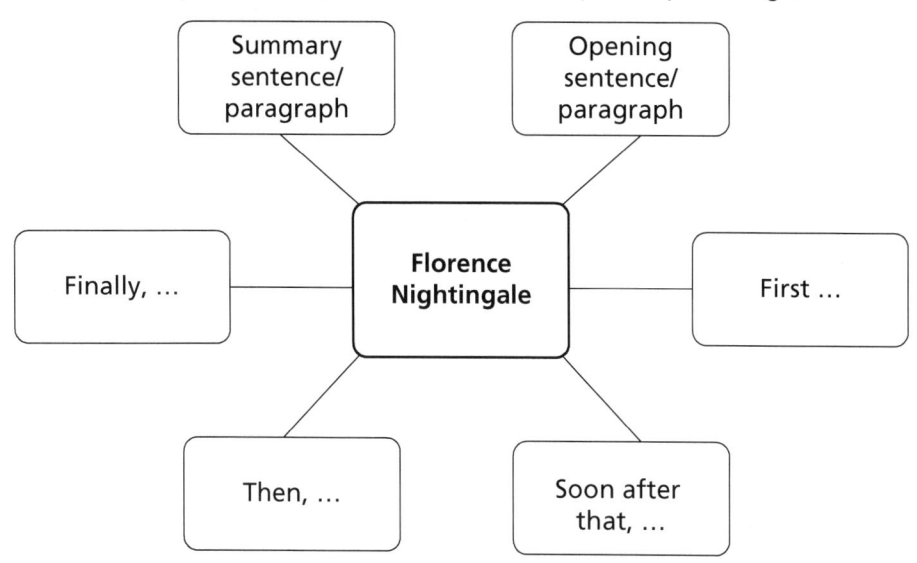

```
    Summary                    Opening
    sentence/                  sentence/
    paragraph                  paragraph

                 Florence
  Finally, ...   Nightingale              First ...

      Then, ...            Soon after
                           that, ...
```

5. Model an opening sentence/paragraph. Start the next paragraph as 'shared writing' by eliciting suggestions from the pupils. Leave both displayed.

6. Pupils write from this point independently or with a partner. Listen to each text. Using peer assessment and the success criteria, evaluate the writing.

7. Pupils self-edit to correct and improve their writing.

Key checks: Are pupils able to use the features of a recount?

Extension: Ask: *Can you make your recount more interesting by including personal opinion?*

Support: Provide a template for a recount (e.g. with time adverbials and memory joggers for each paragraph).

Proofreading to improve

Strand: Writing – composition

Learning objective: To edit by proposing changes to vocabulary, grammar and punctuation in order to enhance effects and clarify meaning.

You will need: whiteboard, passage in step 2 (enlarged), passage containing homophones (step 5), dictionaries, small whiteboards, whiteboard pens

1. **Ask:** *What is proofreading?* Explain that proofreading is when you read your text carefully to spot any mistakes in grammar, punctuation and spelling. You can then edit it by making corrections. **Ask:** *Why is it important to use correct grammar, punctuation and spelling?* Discuss the importance of writing accurately (e.g. in prescriptions, laws, school reports, police reports).

2. Reproduce and enlarge the short passage below; leave out the underlines. Pupils work with a partner and a dictionary to spot and correct the errors.

   william shakespeare was a famus righter. He was born in 1564 in a plaice called stratford-upon-avon before moveing to london wear he worked in the theater. shakespeares audiences wer'ent as well behaved as they are today they would shout and laugh at the actors' or throw food on the stage

3. Display some examples of text messages. **Ask:** *Can you write these in Standard English?* For example:

   (Hiya mate wot RU doin 2nite?
     Mite watch footie at mine.)

4. Provide pupils with sentences containing words spelled with ei or ie. For example:
   - A spider crawled across the ceiling/cieling.
   - Darius is the same hieght/height as me.
   - My sister shrieked/shreiked when she saw the mouse.
   - We learned that eating protein/protien is good for our health.

   Ask: *Can you remember the spelling rule about ie and ei?* **Say:** *i before e, except after c, but only if it rhymes with /ee/. There are exceptions!*

5. Display a short passage containing homophones. **Ask:** *Can you spot the homophones used incorrectly? Write the correct ones.*

Key checks: Do pupils understand the importance of proofreading their work?

Extension: Ask: *Where would you expect to find formal English?*

Support: Underline the words containing errors in steps 2 and 3 and ask pupils to simply correct them.